Self-Love

for KIDS

100+ Activities to Help Your Child Develop Self-Love

KERI K. POWERS,
MA EdHD, MEd, NCC

ADAMS MEDIA
New York   London   Toronto   Sydney   New Delhi

Adams Media
An Imprint of Simon & Schuster, Inc.
100 Technology Center Drive
Stoughton, Massachusetts 02072

First Adams Media trade paperback edition June 2022

ADAMS MEDIA and colophon are trademarks of Simon & Schuster.

For information about special discounts for bulk purchases, please contact Simon & Schuster Special Sales at 1-866-506-1949 or business@simonandschuster.com.

The Simon & Schuster Speakers Bureau can bring authors to your live event. For more information or to book an event contact the Simon & Schuster Speakers Bureau at 1-866-248-3049 or visit our website at www.simonspeakers.com.

Interior design by Sylvia McArdle
Interior layout by Colleen Cunningham
Interior images © 123RF

Manufactured in the United States of America

1 2022

Library of Congress Cataloging-in-Publication Data has been applied for.

ISBN 978-1-5072-1803-7
ISBN 978-1-5072-1804-4 (ebook)

CONTENTS

CHAPTER 4. CONFIDENCE   66

CHAPTER 5. COMPETENCE   89

CHAPTER 6. PURPOSE AND CONTRIBUTION   115

CHAPTER 7. INFLUENCE   138

CHAPTER 8. IDENTITY   155

CHAPTER 9. WORTH   183

CHAPTER 10. PHYSICAL WELL-BEING   214

PART 3. PRACTICAL APPLICATION   245

CHAPTER 11. INCORPORATING SKILLS INTO EVERYDAY LIFE   246

INTRODUCTION

Self-love is an admiration and appreciation of yourself—your personality, identity, preferences, body, beliefs, and more. All parents and caregivers want their children to experience healthy, fulfilling, and lifelong self-love— but how can you nurture it in kids? With play! The 100+ simple games and activities in *Self-Love for Kids* will help you encourage self-love in children, so they are not afraid to make mistakes, explore their identities, or set big goals.

Teaching your young child the importance of self-love early on—at around ages 5–11—offers a wide range of important benefits. Researchers believe that self-love in childhood can help set the foundation for happiness and success in adulthood.

Self-love is a by-product of high self-esteem and is developed by cultivating the following components:

* Security
* Belonging
* Confidence
* Competence
* Purpose and contribution
* Influence
* Identity
* Worth
* Physical well-being

Each chapter in Part 2 of this book will focus on one of those attributes and offer activities that build and practice it. All the activities will include an appropriate age range, a list of materials needed, step-by-step instructions for setting up and completing the activities, and important reflection questions to ask your child. Really focus in on those reflection questions to encourage your child to think about the impact of the activities and to help them look ahead to how they might implement newly learned strategies in everyday life.

These activities can be done in a short amount of time, either at home within your family, with a group of friends on a playdate or in the neighborhood, or even at a distance with family and friends over a video chat. The activities teach kids through imaginative play, hands-on experience, watching others model relevant skills, and person-to-person interaction. Every child is different, so this range of techniques allows you to choose which are best for your child's personality and age as well as the situation at hand.

The activities in this book can help you and your child bond, all while helping them blossom into the beautiful, unique person you know they are. Practicing the self-love skills featured in this book will give your child the emotional intelligence to feel happy and confident at home, at the playground, in the community, at school, and beyond! Let's get started!

UNDERSTANDING SELF-LOVE

In Part 1, we'll explore what self-love actually is and why it's so important for your child, both right now and in the future. The development of self-love has deep roots in self-esteem. You'll learn roughly when and how self-esteem develops, changes, and flourishes in childhood, as well as which factors influence a child's self-esteem. You'll also discover the important components of self-love (such as security, identity, and worth), a list of skills kids will use to develop self-love (such as mindfulness, self-reflection, and problem-solving), and a variety of ways you can teach, mold, and build self-love in kids.

If that feels like a lot of information, it's because it is! But that key foundational background will help you see the importance in each activity that comes later in the book. Understanding the "why" behind each component of the activities will give you better perspective into how you can help your child specifically develop meaningful, loving feelings toward themselves that last a lifetime. Let's dive in and explore all the facets that contribute to self-esteem and self-love!

SELF-LOVE 101

WHAT IS SELF-LOVE?

As mentioned in the introduction, self-love is an admiration and appreciation of yourself—your personality, identity, preferences, body, beliefs, and more. Self-love is a by-product of high self-esteem. When you have a positive sense of self and view yourself as worthy and of value, self-love comes naturally! That's why it is so important to build that solid foundation of self-esteem so that self-love can arise.

"Self-esteem" is a phrase parents and caregivers hear often. "Make sure your child has high self-esteem...but not *too* high." "Do things to boost your child's self-esteem...but don't do *too* much." Parents receive so many mixed messages about how to help their children love themselves. To add to the confusion, there are also many terms that are used interchangeably when discussing self-love, like self-esteem, self-worth, confidence, and self-respect. It's no wonder there are so many books, blogs, and podcasts dedicated to this very topic.

To fully understand what self-love is, it is helpful to define it along with common terms that are often used interchangeably with it.

Each of these terms helps define and contribute to your awareness and evaluation of your worth, value, and capacity for success. But don't get caught up in the semantics; when discussing these things with your child, feel free to just say "self-love" or "self-esteem."

Term	Definition
Self-compassion	How you relate to or treat yourself; the degree to which you are kind and forgiving toward yourself
Self-concept	The perception you have of yourself; the awareness of who you are
Self-confidence	The perception you have about your ability to face challenges, solve problems, and engage with the world
Self-efficacy	Your belief that you can succeed at certain tasks
Self-esteem	Your subjective view of your own worth or value and what you think, feel, and believe about yourself
Self-image	How you see yourself (similar to self-concept)
Self-love	The belief that you are worthy of love, along with the actions and thoughts that demonstrate love and care toward yourself
Self-worth	Your perception of your worth in the world

MEASURING SELF-LOVE

Self-love is measurable and changes over time. It occurs on a spectrum and, like self-esteem, is often described as being high or low. Low self-love and self-esteem are characterized by:

* Low confidence
* A feeling of having little control over one's choices or experiences
* Engaging in negative social comparison
* Not asking for or advocating for needs
* Worry or self-doubt
* Difficulty accepting positive feedback
* Negative self-talk
* Negative outlook or view of the world
* Lack of boundaries
* Engaging in people-pleasing

On the other hand, high self-love and self-esteem are characterized by:

* High confidence
* Engaging in appropriate social comparison or self-comparison
* Standing up for oneself and advocating for needs
* Positive and realistic self-talk
* Positive and realistic outlook and view of the world and self
* Setting and respecting boundaries
* Accepting positive feedback and engaging in appropriate self-evaluation

There are many factors that work together to influence self-esteem and self-love. The following are some of these factors and their impacts.

Factor	Impact
Age	As shown in a study by the University of California, Davis, and King's College, self-love changes over time with age, initially rising in early childhood as cognition and awareness grow. Some people experience dips in adolescence and early adulthood, then an increase in older adulthood. The development of self-love will be discussed at length in a later section.
Socioeconomic status	People with higher socioeconomic status tend to report higher self-esteem. Researchers believe this is related to greater access to resources like physical and mental healthcare and basic needs such as food and shelter consistently being met. The experience of family poverty in childhood is associated with lower self-esteem in adulthood.

Factor	Impact
Genetics	While genes are certainly not the only predictor of self-esteem, there is a genetic component. Researchers from the University of California, Los Angeles, identified a gene that is associated with self-esteem. Outside of a potential self-esteem gene, genetic factors like sex, race, height, weight, and physical appearance also impact self-esteem. In general, males tend to score higher on self-esteem assessments than females. Researchers have also suggested that when African Americans have recent or lifetime experiences of racism, they have higher rates of internalized shame. Internalized shame is negatively associated with self-esteem. However, a study (published in *Journal of Black Studies*) of racial socialization experiences (the degree to which families expose their children to events and stories that reflect pride in their culture) in African-American adolescents suggested that having more positive racial socialization experiences was associated with higher self-esteem in African-American adolescents, while racial socialization messages that focused on the majority culture (white) were associated with lower self-esteem.
Physical abilities or disabilities	The ability to independently do physical tasks associated with daily living, like getting yourself dressed and brushing your teeth, is associated with higher self-esteem. The success experienced in mastering new physical tasks, such as learning to walk or learning a sport, is also associated with higher self-esteem.
Social experiences	Having positive social experiences, such as forming friendships, being a member of a team, or simply successfully engaging in school or the workplace, is associated with higher self-esteem and, therefore, self-love. On the other hand, negative social experiences, such as bullying and racism, are associated with lower self-esteem and self-love.

Factor	Impact
Chronic stress	The experience of stress does not necessarily change a person's sense of self. However, a person's feelings about their capacity to face the challenges or meet the demands of stressful situations are related to self-esteem and self-love. When chronic stress is a result of things like poverty, lack of resources, danger, violence, or basic needs not being met, self-esteem is negatively impacted.
Relationships	Relationships with caregivers set the stage for self-love development early on. Researchers found that when children experienced loving and responsive parenting, cognitive engagement, and a safe, non-chaotic home environment from ages 0–6, they were more likely to have higher self-esteem in adulthood. Peer acceptance and social relationships also impact self-esteem.

When there are so many factors that impact self-love, where should you put your focus when it comes to helping children? On the factors that you can control, of course! While we may not be able to control genetics, physical abilities, or socioeconomic status, we can directly impact the relationships and social experiences that children have in their lives. So as we think about the factors that impact self-love, it's important to take a look at how self-love develops with these factors in mind.

WHY IS SELF-LOVE IMPORTANT?

Self-esteem and self-love impact how we make decisions, the relationships we have and maintain, our emotional health, the risks we take, our motivation, and our overall well-being. People who have high self-love and self-esteem have strong self-awareness regarding their skills and strengths, can form and maintain healthy relationships, have appropriate and realistic expectations of themselves, and are aware of their own personal needs and able to express and share these needs appropriately with others.

Having high self-esteem doesn't just mean someone thinks highly of themselves or has an inaccurate view of their abilities and skills. Actually, people with high self-esteem are more aware of their abilities and skills and demonstrate more self-acceptance. In other words, they know what they're good at and accept themselves for who they are!

Because self-love is based on our opinions and beliefs about ourselves and our place in the world, these opinions and beliefs can be hard to change. But it is imperative that we spend the time to encourage healthy self-love development, because a child's sense of self can determine many things, such as whether kids:

* Like themselves
* Value themselves as people
* Are able to make important decisions
* Are able to assert themselves when necessary
* Can recognize their own strengths, skills, and positive attributes
* Are willing to take small risks, try new things, or attempt things they perceive to be difficult
* Are able to bounce back from mistakes
* Recognize their need for alone time or self-care
* Believe they deserve happiness

Additionally, researchers at the University of Texas at Austin have identified several potential consequences of having low self-esteem. First, long-term effects of low self-esteem include feelings of anxiety, stress, depression, and isolation. Low self-esteem can also result in problems in friendships and romantic partner relationships. Academic and job performance decline with long-term low self-esteem. And finally, low self-esteem increases the likelihood of drug and alcohol abuse. To make matters worse, all these potential consequences can reinforce the negative self-esteem that contributed to them, creating a negative cycle.

HOW AND WHEN DOES SELF-LOVE DEVELOP?

Self-love is a skill that is constantly developing, from birth to adolescence and even well into adulthood. As your child grows, you can expect to see them develop various aspects of self-love. As with most aspects of child development, progress will vary from child to child. Some parts of these skills may show up earlier than expected, and some may appear later. Typically, this isn't cause for alarm, but always reach out to your pediatrician if you have concerns about your child's interactions, behavior, or health.

Infancy

The development of self-love begins right away. This is because having basic needs met is a critical component of self-love development. Infants have a need not only for nourishment and sleep but for love, comfort, closeness, and responsiveness as well. When their needs are met, infants feel safe, secure, and loved. This initial exposure to love, safety, and comfort sets the stage for learning that one is worthy of love.

Toddlerhood

At this stage, children do not have a clear sense of self. However, the toddler years are filled with opportunities for new skill development! As toddlers learn to walk, talk, climb, and impact others, they develop senses of success and confidence, which are related to self-love and self-esteem development. Encouragement from caregivers goes a long way at this stage too. When caregivers are responsive and encouraging to toddlers' new endeavors, toddlers are more likely to believe they will be successful and try new things.

Preschool

If they have not already been in a daycare setting, children at this age usually begin to have new experiences outside their families of origin. These new experiences and relationships with childcare providers and peers play a role in self-love development as well. When kids have received warmth and responsiveness and had their needs met at previous stages, they are better able to separate from primary caregivers for preschool. They also have more opportunities for independence and initiative as they experience the world outside the home. Offering preschoolers opportunities for independence, involving them in decision-making by offering choices, and encouraging them to try new things all contribute greatly to self-esteem and self-love development at this stage of life.

School Age

Entering school is a critical stage of self-esteem development. Success in academic endeavors, engaging with peers and experiencing peer acceptance, and possibly participating in sports or other extracurricular activities all impact how kids view, think about, and feel about themselves and their abilities.

As they learn new academic material, experiencing success with the material will shape the way they feel about themselves as students. Teachers' responses to mistakes in the classroom or children not understanding material also impacts how kids feel about themselves. In classrooms where mistakes are celebrated as a part of the learning process, kids are more likely to take risks, accept themselves, and respond gently to themselves when they do make mistakes. They will also be more likely to speak up when they don't understand the material and ask for help. On the flip side, if students feel like they will be punished or berated for making mistakes, they'll be less likely to speak up when they do need help and less likely to try new things and take risks with academic material. All these experiences impact self-love!

Peer experiences within the school environment are also influential in the development of self-love and self-esteem. When kids develop meaningful, positive social relationships with friends, they see themselves as worthy of friendship. Kids who struggle to develop friendships are more likely to have low levels of self-love. Kids who experience bullying are also more likely to have low self-esteem. However, kids who already have high self-esteem and experience bullying are more likely to assert themselves, stand up to bullies, and report bullying behaviors.

In early adolescence, body image becomes a factor that influences self-love. Adolescents are often concerned about how they are viewed by their peers, and they may compare themselves to societal beauty standards, social media trends, and other depictions in the media. Adolescents who are teased for their appearance or feel that their bodies are not "good enough" in some way are likely to experience low self-love and self-esteem. However, kids who already have high self-esteem are more likely to like the way they look and accept themselves the way they are.

During school age, there are several protective factors that can positively influence kids' self-esteem. According to the University of Texas at Austin, being listened to, being spoken to with respectful words and tone of voice, receiving warmth and attention, having their achievements recognized, and having their mistakes acknowledged and accepted or forgiven contribute to the development of a healthy sense of self.

IMPORTANT COMPONENTS OF SELF-LOVE

As we discussed earlier in this chapter, self-love starts with the belief that you are worthy of love. But it isn't just the belief. Self-love also involves the next step of taking action to *demonstrate* that love and care toward yourself. The act of being loving toward yourself starts with a state of appreciation for yourself that spurs actions that support physical, mental, emotional, social, and spiritual health and growth.

Self-love has several important components, and the activities and games in this book are divided into chapters about each one.

Component	Description
Security	Security means feeling free from danger or harm. Kids feel security when their needs are met. A sense of security develops when kids know what to expect and know that they will be loved and have their physical, mental, and emotional needs taken care of.
Belonging	Belonging is a feeling that results when you experience love, acceptance, and inclusion in a group. A sense of belonging comes from a feeling of comfort that is provided when kids feel seen and valued in a family, social circle, or community group. It's a sense of being a part of something and being a valuable member of that group.
Confidence	Confidence is the belief or assurance in your own abilities, skills, qualities, efforts, and even progress. It's a feeling of steadiness or firmness in oneself. Confidence is a feeling that has resulting actions. Kids are more likely to try new things, ask for help, and fully enjoy the things they love when they are confident.
Competence	Competence is the ability to do things with success or efficiency. Simply put, competence means that someone can do something well. Competence is different from confidence in a key way: Confidence is the *belief* that you can do something, while competence is actually being able to do it. Both are necessary components of self-love.
Purpose and contribution	Having a sense of purpose means that you have a mindset that drives you toward a desired outcome. You have goals in mind and are working toward them. Having a sense of contribution means that you feel like you're giving back and like you are a meaningful part of the group or community.

Component	Description
Influence	Influence is your capacity to produce outcomes, actions, and behaviors in others. Kids can develop a sense of influence early on as they see their behaviors, cries, or silliness impact the behaviors and reactions of the adults around them. As kids grow, they'll have more opportunities for influence, and their caregivers can help them learn how to use it for good!
Identity	Identity is the basis for your sense of self. It encapsulates your beliefs, culture, roles, values, experiences, interests, relationships, memories, and more. In exploring identity, people often pose questions like "Who are you?" and "Who do you want to be?" As kids grow, have new experiences, learn more about their culture, and formulate their own values, beliefs, and interests, they'll have more opportunities to explore their identities.
Worth	A sense of self-worth is a feeling of deserving good things, belonging with others, and deserving love. Self-worth is different from self-esteem in that while self-esteem can be drawn from external influences, achievements, and successes, self-worth comes from within and relies only on internal feelings. A sense of self-worth is associated with an overall positive opinion of oneself and nonjudgment, acceptance, and gentleness toward oneself. To cultivate a sense of self-worth in children, researchers recommend showing unconditional love, positive regard, and respect and giving kids a chance to experience success.
Physical well-being	Physical well-being relates to a balance in the health of body, mind, and spirit. Choices that promote a healthy lifestyle, such as choosing nourishing foods more often; participating in enjoyed forms of movement; and taking in information, messages, and music that positively influence how you feel and think about yourself make up physical well-being. Simply put, physical well-being is about celebrating the amazing things the body can do.

Let's take a look at each category in a little more depth to learn exactly how it relates to self-love.

Security and Self-Love

When kids are provided with an environment that promotes security, they learn and rest assured that their needs will be met. Kids begin to trust that they will be provided with comfort and love when they need it. They know they'll get food, water, or shelter when they're hungry, thirsty, cold, or tired. When kids know their emotional, physical, and mental needs will be taken care of, that sense of security allows them to better explore other aspects of the world. As they experience love through security, they are better able to show love to themselves.

Belonging and Self-Love

Belonging builds on security in that when kids feel they belong in their family or in a social group, they have a sense of security that others will be there for them and support them. The security of knowing that people have your back is quite powerful!

A sense of belonging is positively related to feelings of self-love. When kids have that sense of belonging with group or family members who welcome them and remind them of the ways in which they are valued and supported, they are better able to recognize those positive, lovable qualities within themselves. The sense of security that comes from belonging creates a foundation that self-love can be built upon.

Confidence and Self-Love

Confidence and self-love go hand in hand. Self-awareness and appropriate self-evaluation are necessary for developing a sense of self-love, and they also help kids evaluate their own skills and abilities in order to develop confidence as they try and master new things. As kids become more confident and assured in their own skills, abilities, and qualities, loving themselves comes naturally.

Becoming more confident involves recognizing unique characteristics that make you...you! As kids develop comfort in their own skin and the confidence to be themselves, try new things, and experience success in different areas of their lives, they begin to love those qualities that contribute to their feelings of comfort and the experience of success. Self-love is a by-product of confidence that comes from accepting oneself, showing oneself compassion, and valuing individual differences.

Competence and Self-Love

When kids are competent and successful, they feel satisfied and proud. People who are competent, or have the skills, characteristics, or qualities to accomplish a task, are more likely to be successful. Competence is therefore related to feelings of pride and satisfaction, which promote self-love. When kids feel good about their abilities and the outcomes they achieve with those abilities, they feel good about themselves too.

Helping kids develop competence in a variety of areas can help them approach new tasks, new situations, challenges, and roadblocks with the mindset that they will have positive outcomes and love themselves anyway even when more challenges arise.

Purpose, Contribution, and Self-Love

Having a sense of purpose is closely related to an understanding of your interests, skills, and qualities and the ways those can be used to achieve a meaningful goal. When kids are aware of their skills and appreciate their own qualities and attributes, they feel better about themselves. Furthermore, when they recognize how they can use those skills, qualities, and attributes in meaningful ways to connect to those around them, self-love flourishes, as a greater sense of belonging is fostered. When kids feel like they can contribute to their families, groups, neighborhoods, communities, and world, self-love is a naturally occurring feeling. They feel more connected to those around them and feel a sense of responsibility and pride in providing for those people in meaningful ways. Believing they can contribute to the world around them with their unique and special qualities is vital for kids to develop self-love.

Influence and Self-Love

Feeling as though you have the ability to influence outcomes with and for others is a big responsibility. When kids see that they have the ability to influence the people and the world around them, they feel powerful and important. People who have a big influence over others tend to feel better about themselves than people who feel like they have no control over events around them, especially when they use that power and influence in a positive way.

When children feel good about the positive impact they have on others, they feel good about themselves too. Helping kids develop a sense of positive influence and contribution in their circles will help them feel good about who they are on the inside and how they show that on the outside.

Identity and Self-Love

Self-awareness and self-evaluation give kids a clearer picture of who they are in the world and in relation to others. Understanding who you are and being comfortable in your own values, beliefs, and interests is where identity and self-love intersect. As kids discover more about who they are and think ahead to who they want to become, they'll receive messages from the people and community around them about whether their identity is accepted. When kids feel not only confident in their own identities but also supported by those around them in those identities, they receive the message that they are valuable and worthy of love. Kids internalize this message and translate it to self-love when they can celebrate their own personal identities with the safety of acceptance from those around them.

Worth and Self-Love

Worth is a key concept associated with self-esteem, and it is critical for self-love development. A sense of self-worth means kids value themselves and believe they are worthy of love and good treatment. As they develop a sense of self-worth, they rely less on external encouragement or praise and derive love and value from internal feelings. Kids who feel worthy believe they deserve to be treated well and with respect. When kids believe they are worthy of good things, they are more likely to accept and show love to themselves.

Physical Well-Being and Self-Love

Physical well-being is all about balance. The goal in this category is to help kids learn to make balanced choices that promote a healthy lifestyle to keep them feeling nourished and active. Promoting physical well-being is not about restrictive meal plans or diets and strenuous exercise regimens. Rather, it's about helping kids learn to make balanced choices that promote a healthy view of themselves and the amazing things their bodies can do. Loving your body is one part of self-love.

SKILLS RELATED TO SELF-LOVE

Each of the activities in this book lists key skills that will come into play as kids participate in the game. Following is a list of some of those skills, what they are, how they relate to self-love, and how practicing them benefits kids.

Mindfulness

Mindfulness is the awareness of the present moment. Being mindful involves both acknowledging and accepting your feelings, thoughts, and physical sensations without judgment and without attempts to change them. Mindfulness is a practice that inherently relies on self-awareness, because you must use self-awareness to be mindful. But mindfulness is also a tool that can aid in self-reflection and self-evaluation. Being able to recognize feelings and thoughts while simultaneously not being critical of them is a means for showing yourself love. It is a way to say, "I have feelings, I accept them, and I love myself."

Problem-Solving

Children can use problem-solving through creativity, determination, perseverance, and resilience in order to face new challenges, make mistakes, and try new strategies. Problem-solving is necessary for self-love, as you sometimes need to use creativity to find new ways to show yourself love, and the willingness to try to solve problems for the good of your mental, physical, emotional, social, and spiritual health is a way to show yourself love.

Self-Awareness

Self-awareness is a familiarity with your inner thoughts, feelings, and actions in a particular moment. When kids are self-aware, they are able to recognize their feelings, identify their emotions, and notice how these things impact them and their actions. Self-awareness matters when it comes to self-love because kids need to be able to identify their thoughts, feelings, and actions in order to accept them, manage them, and address them. For example, if children are able to use self-awareness to recognize that they are feeling stressed and overwhelmed, then they can use that information to take action and engage in calming strategies or self-care activities.

Self-Reflection

In self-reflection, kids think back on how they did or how they handled a certain situation. Self-reflection involves taking a moment to think back on their choices, thoughts, and feelings and notice how those things impacted them. Once again, this information can then be used for good. Much like self-evaluation, self-reflection can be used as a tool for growth and building self-love.

Self- or Co-Regulation

Self-regulation is kids' ability to recognize and manage their emotions, thoughts, and choices, even in times of high or intense emotions. Self-regulation is a process that develops across childhood as kids develop a stronger awareness of their own emotions and learn skills to manage those emotions.

In early childhood, adults can help kids develop self-regulation by using co-regulation, which is the process of engaging in awareness and coping strategies together. This looks like taking a break from an activity that is resulting in higher states of emotion to practice strategies to bring the emotional state back down to calm. For example, if a child is feeling angry or frustrated over losing a board game, the parent and child could take a break. First, the parent can notice aloud, "I see your face is red and your fists are clenched. It looks like you are feeling angry. When I am angry, I like to take deep breaths to calm my body. Can we try it together?"

This process of co-regulation (when the adult models calming strategies for the child and participates in the calming process with them) helps kids develop the skills to do this on their own.

HOW CAN CAREGIVERS TEACH SELF-LOVE?

If self-love sounds like a high-stakes matter, it's because it is. Parents and caregivers want kids to value themselves, see themselves as worthy, feel good about their skills and accomplishments, try new things, and love themselves! So what can you do to help your child develop healthy love for themselves?

First, teach them to be their own cheerleader rather than their own critic. For younger kids, you can do this by:

* Being their cheerleader to model this behavior for them
* Offering encouragement
* Building them up with realistic and positive feedback
* Being a source of unconditional warmth, love, and compassion
* Modeling positive self-talk to teach them to speak kindly to themselves
* Helping them learn to question inner criticism by modeling appropriate self-evaluation and realistic self-talk

Second, let kids know that it is always okay to ask for help. Of course, it is important for kids to be independent and do reasonable things for themselves. But when it comes to problems, feelings, and difficult thoughts, reaching out to loved ones, friends, teachers, counselors, and therapists is always okay. Let kids see you ask for help, or tell them how much better you felt after talking to a friend. Normalize the experience of talking to a therapist by letting them know you see one or telling them that seeing a therapist is an option for them if they want it.

Finally, teach kids to practice self-compassion. Model everyday ways of being gentle with yourself by vocally forgiving yourself for mistakes. Let them see you practice self-care and talk about what self-care activities are most protective and rejuvenating for you. Develop family self-care routines to highlight the importance of caring for yourself. Speak compassionately and lovingly to one another so that the outward dialogue they hear at home becomes the internal dialogue they use to speak to themselves.

Not sure what else to do to help your kid develop self-love? You're in the right place. That's what this book is all about. In the next part, you'll find more than one hundred activities you can do with your child to practice building self-love. All will work in a home or family environment; some might also be appropriate for a classroom or small-group setting. It's time to lay the groundwork for self-love with these fun, meaningful, and creative activities that will have your kid feeling fulfilled, seen, heard, and most importantly, loved!

EXERCISES

In this part, you'll find more than one hundred activities that you can do at home, in the neighborhood, in your community, or on a video chat with friends and family to practice these important skills. Each activity includes a suggested age range, a list of helpful materials, skills that the activity focuses on, step-by-step instructions, and any necessary teaching or preparation tasks to complete before the activity. You'll also find discussion questions for after the activity to get kids thinking about how they can transfer their learning to real-life scenarios. These discussion questions are an important transition to help kids process what they've just done and consider how it relates to the world around them. You'll find specific questions tailored to each exercise, but you can always ask additional open-ended questions, like "What was fun/difficult/easy about this activity?"

Keep in mind that the age ranges given are simply suggestions and that kids develop at different rates (and that's okay!). Pick and choose activities that you think will work best for your child. And if an activity doesn't go how you hoped it would the first time, give it another try later. On the other hand, if your child really enjoys any particular activity, feel free to repeat it over and over. Kids love to feel a sense of mastery when they are able to accomplish a task or challenge. Make small changes to keep things interesting, or make it your own by tailoring an activity to your family's interests to really get buy-in from your child.

Most importantly, have fun together!

CHAPTER 2

SECURITY

WHAT IS SECURITY?

Security refers to feeling free from danger or harm. Kids feel security when their needs are met. A sense of security develops when kids know what to expect and know that they will be loved and have their physical, mental, and emotional needs taken care of.

HOW DOES SECURITY RELATE TO SELF-LOVE?

As kids develop a sense of security, they know that their needs will be met. They trust that they'll receive comfort and love when they need it. They know they'll get food, water, or shelter when they're hungry, thirsty, cold, or tired. When kids know their emotional, physical, and mental needs will be taken care of, that sense of security allows them to better explore other aspects of the world. As they experience love through security, they are better able to show love to themselves.

WHAT DOES SECURITY LOOK AND SOUND LIKE?

The outward demonstration of the feeling of security can be seen in how kids respond to caregivers and family members, their willingness to take risks, and how they engage with the environment around them. Some examples of outward demonstrations of security include:

★ Trying new things
★ Trusting others
★ Positive self-evaluations
★ Expressing needs and asking for help

SECURITY IN KID-FRIENDLY TERMS

To explain security to your kid, try saying something like this:

We all have needs. We need food. We need water. We need shelter. And we need love and to feel connected to other people. When we have all those things and when we trust that the people around us will make sure we continue to have those things, we feel secure! "Secure" means that we trust others to keep us safe. We are a family, and we take care of each other. You can trust us and feel secure that we will take care of your needs.

LOOKING AHEAD

In this chapter, you'll find activities to do as a family or group that show your kid you are responsive to their needs and that they can trust in the security of their family or loved ones. You'll also find activities to help kids regulate their emotions, feel comfortable in predictable routines and boundaries, and recognize people and places that provide security in the community.

HUG WAND

We all need an extra hug from time to time! Sometimes, asking for this can be hard, though, especially when emotions are strong. Make a hug wand so that your child can easily show you that they need some extra affection without saying a word. Receiving affirmation and love when they need it most will help kids remember that they are worthy of love, even in difficult moments.

Age Range:	5–7
Skills:	Co-regulation, self-regulation, communication
Materials:	Craft stick or paper straw, construction paper, glue, glitter, any other craft supplies
Number of Participants:	1+
Where to Play:	Inside or outside

BEFORE YOU START
* Let your child know that we all have hard days and that it's okay to ask for some extra affection and love on hard days (and even on easy days!).
* Make sure they know that anytime they show you the hug wand, you'll be happy to give them extra hugs, affection, and attention.

HOW TO PLAY
* Work together to create a hug wand. Construct it with craft supplies such as a craft stick or paper straw, construction paper to make a star or heart, and glue, and decorate it as you'd like.
* Designate a place in your home where the hug wand will be stored.
* When anyone in the family needs an extra hug or some extra attention and affection, they can get the hug wand and show it or wave it near a caregiver to ask for some extra hugs.
* When your child uses the hug wand to ask for extra hugs or affection, take note of the situations that happened beforehand. These will give you a clue about when your child might need some extra attention in the future.

THINKING BACK AND LOOKING AHEAD
* How did you feel after using the hug wand?
* What other situations might be a good time to use the hug wand?

LOOK FOR THE HELPERS

It's important for kids to feel a sense of security at home, but it's also important to feel a sense of security in the community. Go for a drive or walk around your neighborhood to follow the words of Mr. Rogers: "Look for the helpers." As kids develop an understanding that there are people who provide security and safety around them, they are better able to explore other aspects of the world, because they have that sense of security that things will be okay. This gives them the freedom to explore their own interests and skills.

Age Range:	**5–8**
Skills:	**Observation, social awareness**
Materials:	**Paper, writing utensil (optional)**
Number of Participants:	**1+**
Where to Play:	**In the community**

BEFORE YOU START

* Talk about the community helpers who work to make the community a safe place. Let your child know that these people are there to help in a time of need.
* Make a list with your child of people who help in your community, such as emergency medical technicians, firefighters, police officers, lifeguards, crossing guards, security guards, teachers, doctors, nurses, and so on. If you'd like, write the list down and use it as a checklist.
* Remind your child that there are lots of people in the community who work hard to make it a safe and secure place to live.

HOW TO PLAY

* Go for a drive, walk, or bike ride in your community. Purposefully go by places like hospitals, fire stations, and schools.

(continued on next page)

* Identify helpers in the community who work to keep the community safe and healthy.
* If you're using a checklist, pause to let your child check off each helper they see on your outing.

THINKING BACK AND LOOKING AHEAD
* How does each person we spotted help?
* In what situations might you or the community need help from each helper we saw?

....

Turn this activity into a game by creating simple bingo cards! As kids spot community helpers, they can mark off spaces on their bingo cards. See how quickly someone can get a bingo. Celebrate a win with a trip to the library to check out books on community helpers.

....

BREATH CIRCLE

Breathing together is a great way to connect, calm, and regulate. Taking even two minutes to breath in sync together as a family can help kids not only regulate their emotions but also feel secure, safe, and cared for. This special time regulating together will remind kids that they are capable of calm and deserving of special time together. Adding a loving mantra to your breath circle can also serve as a self-love affirmation!

Age Range:	5–8
Skills:	Co-regulation, self-regulation, coping skills
Materials:	None
Number of Participants:	1+
Where to Play:	Inside or outside

BEFORE YOU START

* Demonstrate for your child what slow, deep breaths look like. Model the slow inhale and slow exhale for them.

HOW TO PLAY

* Sit together on the floor in a circle or across from each other.
* If sitting in a circle, everyone should place their palms against the palms of the people on either side of them. If there are just two people, place both palms against each other's palms while facing each other.
* Take a deep breath in and slowly raise your palms up in the air, counting to 5.
* Slowly blow the breath out while slowly dropping your palms back down, counting to 7. Keep your palms connected throughout the whole breath!
* Continue this for ten breaths.
* Remind kids that you can help them take a moment to breathe whenever they need a moment to regulate and calm down or just to connect.

(continued on next page)

THINKING BACK AND LOOKING AHEAD

★ How did you feel after we finished breathing? (You can describe your own body to help them tune in to their own with phrases like "My heart feels slow and calm" or "My brain feels clear, and my body feels calm.")

★ When might you want to try this breathing exercise in the future?

....

An affirmation is a short, positive statement that can offer support and encouragement. As you finish your breath circle, close out with a self-love affirmation. Try one of these:

• I am worthy of love.

• I am strong and powerful like my breath.

• When I inhale, I remember I am worthy. When I exhale, I remember I am loved.

....

PERSONAL SHIELD

Shield up! What people, things, and words can help kids get through hard times? Making a personal shield to remind them of the things in their life that help them can ensure that they feel safe and protected in any scenario.

Age Range:	5–9
Skills:	Creativity, self-reflection, gratitude
Materials:	Paper, coloring utensils, craft supplies for decorating
Number of Participants:	1+
Where to Play:	Inside

BEFORE YOU START

★ Talk about what a shield is and does. A shield is something people use to protect themselves. We have things in our lives that protect us during hard times too. People, favorite things, and encouraging words can help us feel safe and protected when we go through difficult moments.

HOW TO PLAY

★ On paper, have your child draw a shield. Help younger kids if needed.
★ Separate the shield into three sections.
  • In one section, help your child write the names of people who support them or people who can help them through hard times, such as "Mom and Coach."
  • In another section, help your child write or draw comforting items, places, or activities that help them feel better or safe, such as "my stuffed hedgehog" or "my journal" or "sitting under my favorite tree."
  • In the third section, help your child write affirmations or encouraging words they can say to themselves to remind them of their security when they go through hard times, such as "I am a problem solver" or "It's okay to ask for help."
★ Let your child decorate their shield however they like!

(continued on next page)

THINKING BACK AND LOOKING AHEAD

★ How do these people help you through hard times?
★ How do these items, places, or activities give you comfort?
★ How do these words help you?
★ How can I remind you to use these things and words from your shield when you go through hard times?

POWER PIZZA

Your child is a unique and awesome person full of unique and awesome ingredients! In this activity, you'll work with your child to make a pizza to show off their unique qualities. Helping them think about what makes them amazing will help them feel secure in their worth and value.

Age Range:	**5–9**
Skills:	**Creativity, self-awareness, self-reflection**
Materials:	**White paper or construction paper, coloring utensils, scissors, glue or tape**
Number of Participants:	**1+**
Where to Play:	**Inside**

BEFORE YOU START

★ Talk about how each person has unique and different skills and qualities. It's like our skills and qualities are special ingredients that make us who we are. Celebrating our unique qualities can remind us that we deserve love and we are strong and safe.

HOW TO PLAY

★ Draw a large circle on white paper or cut out a circle from construction paper.
★ Draw another slightly smaller circle inside the circle to create a "crust" for your pizza.
★ Draw lines to divide the circle into four "slices," like a pizza. On the crust for each slice, write:
  • Qualities
  • Skills
  • Words from My Heart
  • Words for My Heart
★ On each slice of the pizza, draw circles like pepperoni or shapes like mushrooms or other toppings. Or, cut the shapes out of extra paper and glue or tape them on.

(continued on next page)

- For the "Qualities" slice, brainstorm words that represent qualities the child has. These could be things like "kind," "creative," "thoughtful," or "athletic." Write them on the toppings on this slice.
- For the "Skills" slice, brainstorm skills the child has. These could be things like "great painter," "helpful friend," or "good speller." Write them on the toppings on this slice.
- For the "Words from My Heart" slice, brainstorm affirmations that the child could say to themselves to remind them of their worth. These could be things like:
  - "I can do hard things."
  - "I love my creative spirit."
  - "I have good ideas."
- For the "Words for My Heart" slice, brainstorm things the child enjoys hearing from others or words that make the child feel loved and write them on the toppings. These could include things like:
  - "I love you."
  - "You're doing a great job."
  - "You're so helpful!"
  - "I love spending time with you."
- Color the pizza and hang it somewhere highly visible so your child can see it often.

THINKING BACK AND LOOKING AHEAD
- What was it like to think about your unique qualities?
- What was it like to think about your unique skills?
- How often do you say these affirmations to yourself? How can I help you remember to say these kind words to yourself?
- Was it easy or hard to think about words that you like to hear from others? Do I say these to you often? What would you like to hear from me more often?
- How will you feel when you look at your pizza later?

CALM CORNER

Understanding that all emotions are normal, expected, and acceptable goes a long way in helping kids feel more comfortable in their own skin. When kids are given space to reflect on, understand, and work through emotions, they become more accepting of themselves and more loving toward themselves. In this activity, you'll create a safe place in your home for kids to process and regulate their emotions so that they can emerge feeling calm, comfortable, and confident.

Age Range:	5–9
Skills:	Co-regulation, self-regulation, coping skills, problem-solving
Materials:	A semiprivate space (like a corner, space under the stairs, or closet space) stocked with comforting items, such as comfortable seating or pillows, stuffed animals, a weighted blanket, noise-canceling headphones, sequined pillows, a sound machine, a timer, coloring materials, journaling materials, differently textured items (like sensory balls or a textured board), a feelings poster or deck of feelings cards, bubbles or pinwheels (for controlled-breathing practice)
Number of Participants:	1
Where to Play:	Inside

BEFORE YOU START

★ Remember that extra time spent teaching and practicing this process when your child is calm and regulated will go a long way in helping your child when they actually have big feelings. Having a routine in place will make it easier for your child to access these skills and the process when they are struggling to regulate themselves. Use encouraging language, such as:
  • We all have big feelings. It's okay to feel them.
  • I am here with you. We will sort this out together.
  • I love you and all your feelings.
  • You have what it takes to handle these feelings. I'll be right here with you.

(continued on next page)

HOW TO PLAY

★ Along with your child, identify a location in your home for a calming space. This could be a corner of a room, a cozy space under the stairs, inside an indoor kids' tent, or even on one side of a closet. This should be a space where kids can feel safe and comfortable but not completely isolated. This space is a place for regulation, not a place for punishment. Note: If you do not have space available for this, you can fill a basket or small tub with comforting items, and this can be taken to a comfortable place when needed.

★ Identify items that are comforting to your child. These can be favorite stuffed animals, pictures of family, a favorite journal, or anything else that helps your child feel calm and secure. Place these items in the space or in a basket in the space.

★ Hang a feelings poster in the space or place a deck of feelings cards there (you can find these online to print at home or purchase them premade from your favorite children's toy retailers).

★ Spend 5–15 minutes in this calm space daily with your child. Using the space together will normalize the experience as well as give your child a sense of safety in identifying feelings and using strategies to feel better. Practice identifying feelings using your feelings poster or cards. Practice using the calming items you've included in the space. This might look like:

- Both of you enter the calm space together and set a timer for the amount of time you'd like to spend there that day.
- Both of you sit in the calm space and take ten deep breaths. This can be done simply by breathing together or by using a pinwheel or bubbles for a visual representation of breathing.
- Both of you take turns naming how you feel at the moment. "Right now I feel happy," or "Right now I feel sad. This feeling is temporary."
- Take 3–10 minutes to practice using the items in the calming space. Depending on the age of your child, you may choose to practice using one item per day for a few days. Take time to write in a journal or silently graze your hands over a sequined pillow.
- At the end of your time in the calm space, identify how you are feeling again. "Now I am feeling calm," or "Right now I feel loved."

★ When your child has big feelings that require a moment to regulate (e.g., they are feeling angry, frustrated, sad, or overwhelmed), enter the calm space together. Complete the same sequence of events that you have practiced before. Model the regulation strategies for your child together and stay with them as they regulate their feelings.

* After you've gone through this process together a few times, your child may feel more confident to enter the space and regulate on their own in the future. Make the space available at all times so that your child knows that it's okay to have big feelings and to take time to use appropriate strategies to feel better.

THINKING BACK AND LOOKING AHEAD
* How are you feeling after using your calm space?
* Which of the items in your calm space is most calming for you?
* How could you use some of these calming strategies if you feel upset when you are not home?
* Which feelings are easiest for you to manage on your own?
* Which feelings do you need my help with?
* What else could we add to your space to help you feel safe?

Give your calm space a special name! Need some inspiration? You could call it the Calm Corner, Chill Zone, Rest Nest, Zen Den, or Regulation Station—or see what your child comes up with. Giving them the freedom and ownership to name their space will give them a sense of agency, which is self-esteem boosting in itself! Create a sign or label for your space with your child's favorite art supplies.

HOME BASE

Whether everyone in the home goes to different places during the day or stays home to work and learn, having a predictable home base to come to for rest, comfort, and reflection is a great way to instill a sense of security in your child. Setting aside special, consistent "home base time" each day will help your child know that no matter what the day holds, a comfortable and safe place to land awaits at the end of the day. As kids experience the comfort, acceptance, and love that comes during special home base time, those feelings will translate into self-comfort, self-acceptance, and self-love.

Age Range:	5–11
Skills:	Co-regulation, self-regulation, coping skills, communication
Materials:	Blankets, stuffed animals, pillows (optional)
Number of Participants:	1+
Where to Play:	In a special, consistent spot, such as the living room or the child's bedroom

BEFORE YOU START

* Choose a time that will be easy to stick to. Maybe your time is right after dinner or just before bed. Just make sure it is a time that can be consistent daily.
* Decide on a location for your home base activity. Choose a spot that is always accessible. If one parent sometimes takes business calls in the parents' bedroom in the evening, choose a child's room or the living room instead.

HOW TO PLAY

* Work together to designate a consistent time each day when you will do this activity. It's important that it's an activity that kids know to expect and know they can count on to happen.
* Come together with your child for home base time. This can be a time for end-of-day snuggles, reflecting on the day, or sharing thoughts together, depending on your child's age. Bring your child's favorite

blanket, stuffed animal, or pillow and snuggle together as you talk or sing. Spend time with your child cuddling, singing, talking, or laughing, giving your child a sense of a secure, dependable home base.

* The time is all about togetherness, so no phones or other distractions should be in the room.

* End your home base time with a consistent closing ritual. For younger children, you can sing a favorite song; for older children, say a simple phrase, such as, "I'm so glad I get to end my day with you!"

* As your child gets older, they may want to direct some of the home base time by adding their own questions or activities. That's okay! This means they feel secure enough to propose a change. The key is for the child to feel calm and open during home base time. If they do not, make small changes to your time so that it feels like a calm, safe space to open up, unwind, and relax.

THINKING BACK AND LOOKING AHEAD

* How do you feel when we spend time together at the end of each day?
* Is there anything we can do during this time to help you feel safer?
* Is there anything else you want me to know about your day?

MAKE YOUR HOME A SAFE ZONE

Home should feel like a safe place for everyone to be themselves. In this activity, you'll work together as a family unit drafting "Safe Zone" rules, or guidelines that let the whole family know how to treat one another so that the safe space at home can feel welcoming, inviting, and comfortable for everyone. Creating Safe Zone rules will give everyone in the family not only the understanding of the expectations but also a sense of comfort, belonging, acceptance, and love. These rules serve as a reminder that everyone is accepted just as they are, which promotes feelings of self-love.

Age Range:	**5–11**
Skills:	**Collaboration, communication, acceptance, respect**
Materials:	**Paper, writing utensils**
Number of Participants:	**The whole family**
Where to Play:	**In a quiet, comfortable place free from distractions**

BEFORE YOU START

★ Think about rules you as a caregiver definitely want to include in the Safe Zone, then think of ways to prompt kids to generate these ideas on their own. When they come up with the rules themselves, they're more likely to stick to them! For example, if you want to create a rule that everyone is called by their name or nickname (i.e., no name-calling), you might ask, "And what should we call each other when we speak to each other?"

HOW TO PLAY

★ Call a family meeting. Everyone in the household should attend with no distractions. Leave cell phones in another room and turn off tablets and TVs.

★ Let kids know that home is a Safe Zone where they can feel comfortable and safe to be fully themselves.

* Work together to create Safe Zone rules. These rules will help everyone know how to treat one another so that they can really feel like home is a safe place. These rules should be phrased in a positive tone. For example, a rule might be, "Call everyone by their given name or a nickname that they like," instead of, "No name-calling." Phrasing rules in the positive tells kids what to do instead of what not to do.
* Let kids and adults suggest rules, and then talk about them as a family. If everyone agrees on a rule, write it on the paper.
* Think about how you want to handle it when rules are broken. This may be part of the conversation in this first meeting, or you may want to have this discussion later. Kids should know exactly what the expectations are and what the consequences are for breaking these rules.
* When you are finished creating your Safe Zone rules, everyone should sign the list of rules as a commitment to following these guidelines so that everyone in the family feels comfortable and safe to be their real selves at home.
* Chances are, things might happen later that will have the family thinking a new rule is needed. That's okay! Call another family meeting to discuss potential new rules for the Safe Zone.

THINKING BACK AND LOOKING AHEAD
* Which of these guidelines do you think is most important?
* How should we remind each other to stick to these?
* How do you feel knowing these guidelines are in place?

VISUAL SCHEDULE

Kids thrive and feel secure when they know what to expect. Create a visual schedule for the day or week that they can reference frequently. The sense of security that comes from knowing what to expect will help kids feel prepared, confident, and in the know.

Age Range:	**5–11**
Skills:	**Preparedness, time management**
Materials:	**Paper, scissors, markers, magnets or another way to display the schedule, glue**
Number of Participants:	**1+**
Where to Play:	**Inside**

BEFORE YOU START

★ When you know ahead of time that there will be changes to the regular schedule, let kids know. Knowing what to expect, even if it's different, will give them a sense of security.

HOW TO PLAY

★ Together with your child, make a list of all the activities that the family does on any given day.
★ For younger kids, decide what symbol or picture could represent each activity. For example:
  • Get dressed: Shirt
  • Brush teeth: Toothbrush
  • Eat breakfast: Cereal box
  • Pack backpack: Backpack
  • Do homework: Book and pencil
★ Cut out strips of paper, then draw (or print out) pictures of the chosen symbols and write the activities. You may want to laminate these strips of paper for longevity.
★ Each day, display the daily schedule using these strips of paper. You can hang them on the refrigerator with magnets or on a poster board with hook-and-loop material such as Velcro brand.

* Review the daily schedule in the morning so that everyone knows what to expect for the day.
* If you'd like, you or your child can remove each strip of paper or cross off each activity as it is completed.

THINKING BACK AND LOOKING AHEAD

* Which of these routines is your favorite?
* Which of these routines is hardest for you? How can I help?
* Is there anything fun you would like to have included in our routine?

Older kids might work well viewing the day's events on a whiteboard calendar instead of a paper version. They can color-code different activities in different marker colors or use magnets to represent certain events.

CHAPTER 3

BELONGING

WHAT IS BELONGING?

Belonging is a feeling of security that results when kids experience love, acceptance, and inclusion in a group. A sense of belonging comes from a feeling of comfort that is provided when children feel seen and valued in a family, social circle, or community group. It's a sense of being a part of something and being a valuable member of that group.

HOW DOES BELONGING RELATE TO SELF-LOVE?

A sense of belonging is positively related to feelings of self-love. When children have group or family members who welcome them and remind them of the ways in which they are valued and supported, they are better able to recognize those positive, lovable qualities within themselves. The sense of security that comes from belonging creates a foundation that self-love can be built upon.

WHAT DOES BELONGING LOOK AND SOUND LIKE?

The outward demonstration of the feeling of belonging can be seen in a child's willingness to be open, share pieces of themselves, and show others their real self. Some examples of outward demonstrations of belonging include:

⋆ Joining a group
⋆ Participating in group activities
⋆ Sharing feelings and ideas within the group
⋆ Going to the group or members of the group for comfort and help
⋆ Being willing to take risks in the group, knowing that they will be accepted whether they are successful or not

BELONGING IN KID-FRIENDLY TERMS

To explain belonging to your kid, try saying something like this:

> We are a family. Each one of us has a special place in our family and adds to our family in amazing ways! You will always fit with us. We will always accept you. We will always love you. We want you to know that your unique qualities, your special skills, your amazing ideas, and your fun interests will always be welcome with us. You belong with us! "Belonging" means that you fit and we are here to help you grow and support you.

LOOKING AHEAD

In this chapter, you'll find activities to do as a family or group that show your kid that they belong and that they are an important and valuable member. You'll also find a few activities that help kids recognize how they belong in other areas, like your neighborhood, community, and social groups.

GUESS WHO

Get together for a guessing game...with a twist! Give clues about how a family or group member fits into or contributes to the whole unit, and let others guess who it is. This activity helps reinforce unity and belonging, which build self-love.

Age Range:	**5–8**
Skills:	**Respect, kindness, social contribution, creativity**
Materials:	**Paper, writing utensil, bowl or hat**
Number of Participants:	**The whole family or group**
Where to Play:	**Inside or outside**

BEFORE YOU START

★ Talk about how each member of the family or group contributes in their own special way. You might mention things like:
  • Mom works really hard at her job so that we can have things we need.
  • Dad is so good at making healthy food for us.
  • Konner makes us laugh with his silly jokes.
  • Hanna encourages us with kind words.

HOW TO PLAY

★ Write each person's name on a strip of paper and place them in a bowl or hat.
★ Take turns drawing one name from the bowl. (If someone gets their own name, they should put it back and draw again.)
★ The person who chose a name gives clues about how the person on the paper contributes to and fits into the group and makes it better. All clues should be positive.
★ Other participants will guess who is listed on the paper.
★ When the person is guessed, another participant chooses a piece of paper and gives clues.

THINKING BACK AND LOOKING AHEAD

* How did it feel to think of the special qualities of others?
* How did it feel to hear your own special qualities?
* How do all our special qualities work together to make our family or group amazing?

WHERE I FIT

Show the ways each member uniquely shines within the group or family unit while still fitting together by creating a group puzzle. This activity reinforces a sense of belonging for everyone, highlighting how each person has a special place and fits with the others. Seeing their unique qualities, skills, and interests fitting in to make a beautiful puzzle will promote a sense of value and self-love in your child.

Age Range:	**5–11**
Skills:	**Cooperation, creativity**
Materials:	**Paper, scissors, markers, coloring utensils, pencils, card stock and glue (optional), picture frame (optional)**
Number of Participants:	**The whole family or group**
Where to Play:	**Inside**

BEFORE YOU START

★ Take a large piece of paper and cut it into a puzzle. Each person in the family or group should have one piece of the puzzle.

★ Talk about the ways each person "fits" into the group. Discuss the qualities and strengths each person has or ways they contribute to the group and the ways in which these unique qualities make your group special as a whole unit. For example, you might say, "You always make everyone smile with your good morning song!" or "Your curiosity helps us all learn more and look at things in new ways."

HOW TO PLAY

★ Each participant will decorate one puzzle piece in their own unique way to represent themselves. They can use symbols to represent things they love or their personality traits, or they can decorate it with patterns or their favorite colors.

★ When everyone's puzzle piece is finished, take turns sharing why the piece was decorated in the way it was.

* Put all the pieces together. You may want to mount it on card stock or another type of sturdy paper. Frame your puzzle or display it as a reminder of the way you all fit together!

THINKING BACK AND LOOKING AHEAD

* Reflect on your family puzzle together.
  * What is it like to see all the pieces together?
  * How does it feel to know we fit together?
  * How can we remind one another that we all have a special place in the family?

GRATITUDE CIRCLE

Taking time to express gratitude for one another promotes feelings of belonging, security, and connection. Tell other people in your group or family why you're grateful for all the things they do, say, and are. Hearing why others are grateful for them will help kids internalize their contributions and value, promoting self-love.

Age Range:	5–11
Skills:	Respect, kindness, support
Materials:	None
Number of Participants:	The whole family or group
Where to Play:	In a comfortable spot with limited distractions

BEFORE YOU START

* Review what it means to be grateful. It means that we appreciate someone or something and that someone or something makes our lives better.
* Give examples of reasons we might be grateful for someone, such as:
  * We appreciate something they did or do.
  * We appreciate a quality they have.
  * We appreciate how they treat us.
  * We appreciate how they take care of things.

HOW TO PLAY

* Sit together as a family or group in a circle. Begin by saying together, "We are grateful for each other!"
* To start, have one person be the focal person. Everyone else will take turns offering one or two reasons why they are grateful for that focal person.
* Repeat with each person until everyone has been the focal person and heard why everyone else is grateful for them.

THINKING BACK AND LOOKING AHEAD

* How did it feel to share why you're grateful for others?
* How did it feel to hear why others are grateful for you?
* How would things be different if we shared why we're grateful each day?

FAMILY CREST

Create a visual representation of the guiding principles of your family with this creative activity. Seeing a family crest displayed each day will remind kids they belong to the family unit. This sense of belonging and unity will contribute to a healthy development of self-love as kids see themselves live out the ideals of the family unit.

Age Range:	**5–11**
Skills:	**Collaboration, cooperation, creativity**
Materials:	**Paper, pencils, drawing utensils like markers, art supplies, card stock or cardboard, picture frame (optional)**
Number of Participants:	**The whole family**
Where to Play:	**Inside**

BEFORE YOU START
* If you'd like, compile a list of positive qualities or attributes that you want to guide your family toward.
* If applicable, ask older children to review the list and think about which three or four are most important to them. They can share their reasoning with the whole family when you come together.

HOW TO PLAY
* Draw a large shield or crest.
* Write the family name on the crest. If all family members do not have the same last name, choose a family name or team name that everyone agrees on.

(continued on next page)

* Talk about symbols that represent who the family is or what qualities you want to have. For example, you may choose symbols such as:

Quality	Symbol
Loyalty	Knot
Trustworthiness	Handshake
Kindness	Heart
Supportiveness	Anchor
Fun	Silly face

* Choose three or four symbols to include on the shield. Work together to draw, color, and decorate them on the family crest.
* Mount it on card stock or cardboard, then frame it or display it somewhere in the home.

THINKING BACK AND LOOKING AHEAD

* What is it like to look at our family crest?
* What will you think of when you look at it each day?
* How will it impact your choices?

FAMILY MOTTO

What's your family motto? Get together to create a family motto to bond you together. A shared motto can create a sense of belonging and unity that will contribute to self-love as kids feel connected to the family unit.

Age Range:	**5–11**
Skills:	**Collaboration, cooperation, creativity**
Materials:	**Paper, writing utensil**
Number of Participants:	**The whole family**
Where to Play:	**Inside**

BEFORE YOU START

★ Talk about what a motto is. A motto is a short sentence or phrase that expresses the beliefs or guiding principles of a person or group.
★ Talk about what your family's guiding principles are. What sorts of things do you believe? What actions or qualities do you value? How do you want to represent yourself and your family?

HOW TO PLAY

★ Together, create a short family motto that's one sentence or phrase. This motto should state who you are as a family, how you treat one another, or what principles you want to live by.
★ Here are a few examples:
  • We are kind, we are trustworthy, and we work together!
  • The Phillips family sticks together!
  • Be respectful, be helpful, be curious!
★ Write your family motto on paper and hang it somewhere visible.
★ Repeat your family motto together at important times, like before a trip, before bed, or when the family faces challenges.

THINKING BACK AND LOOKING AHEAD

★ How does it feel to say our family motto?
★ Which part of the motto means the most to you?
★ How do you think our family motto will guide you?
★ At what times do you think we should say our family motto together?

SAME, SAME, DIFFERENT

Family members have a lot in common—but they also have individual differences that make them special and unique. Explore ways that you are similar but different to celebrate togetherness, belonging, and uniqueness. Highlighting shared qualities and unique differences will help kids feel bonded to the family while still honoring their unique and special qualities, which will help them feel a sense of self-love.

Age Range:	**5–11**
Skills:	**Respect, cooperation, creativity**
Materials:	**None**
Number of Participants:	**The whole family**
Where to Play:	**Inside or outside**

BEFORE YOU START

* If you'd like (and if applicable), give kids who can write time to make a list of things they like, qualities they have, or facts about themselves before you start.
* Remind everyone that family members will have some similarities, but it's okay to have differences too!

HOW TO PLAY

* One person will say something that is true about them. It could be a favorite color, a favorite sports team, a characteristic, or something else.
* Other family members will take turns saying "Same" if they share that interest or quality or "Different" if they have a different interest or quality. You could also use one hand signal for "Same" and another for "Different" to add movement to the activity.
* Continue until everyone has had several turns.

THINKING BACK AND LOOKING AHEAD

* How did you feel when others said, "Same"?
* How did you feel when others said, "Different"?
* How do you think having common interests or qualities helps us as a family?
* How do you think having different interests or qualities helps us as family?
* Did anyone have an interest that was different from yours that you might like to learn more about?

FAMILY HANDSHAKE

Kids probably see professional athletes doing special handshakes on television. Make up your own family handshake to have a special way to greet each other, celebrate, or say goodbye. This shared special gesture can build cohesion and a sense of unity that will contribute to self-love as kids feel connected to the family unit.

Age Range:	5–11
Skills:	Cooperation, creativity
Materials:	None
Number of Participants:	The whole family
Where to Play:	Inside or outside

BEFORE YOU START

★ If handshakes are new to your kid, spend some time looking up handshake videos online. Searching "teacher student handshakes" will give you some great inspiration.

HOW TO PLAY

★ Work together to make up your own family handshake that everyone can do. If you have multiple children with a wide age range, make a handshake that even the littlest family member can do.
★ Practice it together!
★ Make a plan for when you might do your family handshake. It could be a morning ritual, a goodbye ritual, or something you do to celebrate big accomplishments.

THINKING BACK AND LOOKING AHEAD

★ How does it feel to have a family handshake?
★ How do you think you'll feel when we do it during one of the times we decided on?
★ Which part of the handshake is your favorite? Why?

FAMILY VISION BOARD

Time to break out the craft supplies! Look into the future: What do we see for our family? What do we want to be? How do we want to be living? Create a vision board to show off the family's dreams. This collaborative effort of looking ahead will help kids feel like they are contributing to the family unit with a sense of purpose. This feeling of belonging will add to their feelings of self-love!

Age Range:	5–11
Skills:	Collaboration, cooperation, creativity
Materials:	Poster board, markers, magazines, scissors, glue
Number of Participants:	The whole family
Where to Play:	Inside

BEFORE YOU START

* Explain what a vision board is. It is a place where you can record your goals, dreams, and aspirations so you can all see them whenever you want. You can use it for inspiration when you're trying to decide what actions to take or to remember what your priorities are as a family.
* Talk about your goals as a family. What are some things you want to do more of? What are the ways you want to treat the family? Others outside the family?

HOW TO PLAY

* Divide the poster board into four sections. In the middle, write, "Our Family Vision Board."
* Label the four sections:
  * Things We Love to Do Together
  * Things We Want to Do More Often
  * How We Want to Treat Each Other
  * How We Want to Treat Our Neighbors and Community

(continued on next page)

* For each section, work together to cut out pictures from magazines, draw pictures or symbols, or write words that best represent how the family feels about each topic.
* Here is an example:

Our Family Vision Board	
Things We Love to Do Together * Make pancakes on Saturday * Go for bike rides after dinner * Play card games	**Things We Want to Do More Often** * Go hiking * Have movie nights * Paint
How We Want to Treat Each Other * Listen before we speak * Work out problems * Stand up for each other	**How We Want to Treat Our Neighbors and Community** * Invite our neighbors over * Clean up the beach * Volunteer

* Hang your family vision board somewhere highly visible in your home so you can check in throughout the year or reference it as needed.

THINKING BACK AND LOOKING AHEAD

* How does it feel to see all of our family's goals or aspirations in one place?
* When you look at our vision board in the future, how will it motivate you?
* How do you think we should use this vision board?
* Which thing on our vision board are you most excited about?

CIRCLE OF SUPPORT

In this activity, kids will think about the people in their lives who support them in and out of the home. Having a visual representation of the people in their lives who offer support will remind kids of how they belong to a family, community, or group and help them remember they are deserving of love.

Age Range:	**5–11**
Skills:	**Respect, reflection**
Materials:	**Paper, pencils, coloring utensils, glue, picture of your child, pictures of family members, supportive neighbors, and friends**
Number of Participants:	**1+**
Where to Play:	**Inside**

BEFORE YOU START
* Talk about what it means to be supportive.
* Ask your child to name people who support them at home, in the neighborhood, at school, or in other places where they spend time.

HOW TO PLAY
* On the top of a piece of paper, write, "My Circle of Support." Draw a small circle in the middle of the paper. Glue a picture of your child in the center or let your child draw a picture of themselves.
* Outside the circle, glue pictures of family members, supportive neighbors, and friends, or let your child draw a picture of each person. You can also have your child draw a symbol to represent each person.
* When your child is finished, ask them to share how each person supports them.
* Have your child say or think, "I belong with all these people!"

THINKING BACK AND LOOKING AHEAD
* How do you feel seeing all the people who support you?
* How does it feel to know you belong and are accepted by all these people?
* How do you like to be supported by others?

CHAPTER 4

CONFIDENCE

WHAT IS CONFIDENCE?

Confidence is the belief or assurance that kids have in their own abilities, skills, qualities, efforts, and even progress. It's a feeling of steadiness or firmness in themselves. Confidence is a feeling that has resulting actions. Children are more likely to try new things, ask for help, and fully enjoy the things they love when they are confident.

HOW DOES CONFIDENCE RELATE TO SELF-LOVE?

Confidence and self-love are very closely related. As kids become more confident and assured in their own skills, abilities, and qualities, loving themselves comes naturally. Becoming more confident involves recognizing unique characteristics that make you special just as you are. As kids develop comfort in their own skin and the confidence to be themselves, try new things, and experience success, they are more likely to love those qualities that contribute to their feelings of comfort and the experience of success. Self-love is a by-product of confidence that comes from accepting yourself, showing yourself compassion, and valuing individual differences.

WHAT DOES CONFIDENCE LOOK AND SOUND LIKE?

The outward demonstration of confidence involves speaking up for yourself, asking for help when needed, and stepping outside your comfort zones with the assurance that your skills, practice, and qualities will contribute to success. Some examples of outward demonstrations of confidence include:

* Standing up straight with shoulders back and head up
* Making eye contact
* Trying new things
* Taking small risks to achieve goals

* Speaking clearly or excitedly
* Speaking positively about yourself
* Accepting yourself
* Showing compassion to yourself
* Asking for help

CONFIDENCE IN KID-FRIENDLY TERMS

To explain confidence to your kid, try saying something like this:

You are going to try so many new things in your life! Sometimes, those things will be easy, and you'll get them right away. Sometimes, things might feel hard. But confidence is something that can help you face hard things or try new, unfamiliar things. "Confidence" means that you believe in yourself. It means that you know you have special skills and abilities that will help you be successful, and it means that you can be brave to try new things.

LOOKING AHEAD

In this chapter, you'll find activities that encourage kids to step outside their comfort zones and take risks with confidence. You'll also find activities that help kids recognize their own strengths through the eyes of others, believe in their abilities to try new things, and overcome challenges.

FLYING HIGH

Capes aren't just for superheroes—they can be for any child who wants to feel confident. A cape can offer a sense of security, and along with words of encouragement, it can offer a confidence boost as well! Grab some markers and create a confidence cape so your child can fly high with confidence.

Age Range:	**5–8**
Skills:	**Creativity**
Materials:	**Large piece of paper or old sheet or pillowcase, markers or paint, masking tape**
Number of Participants:	**1+**
Where to Play:	**Inside or outside**

BEFORE YOU START

★ Talk about words of encouragement. You might say something like, "Words of encouragement are things we can say to help others feel confident and brave." Here are some questions to ask kids to prompt discussion about encouragement:
  • What words make you feel good?
  • What can people say to help you feel like you can do hard things or face challenges?
  • What can you say to others to encourage them?

HOW TO PLAY

★ Give your child a piece of paper large enough to fit on their back. Alternately, you can use an old sheet or pillowcase.
★ On the paper or sheet, other children will write words of encouragement or draw encouraging pictures. If working alone, you can write encouraging words or the child can write these things themselves. The adult can help younger children spell or write the words as needed. For example, they might write:
  • You've got this!
  • You can do hard things!
  • I am strong and brave!

* Let your child decorate their cape in between the words of encouragement.
* Help your child make a cape out of the paper or sheet so they can wear their confidence cape. Tape the cape to your child's shirt with masking tape.

THINKING BACK AND LOOKING AHEAD

* What thoughts do you have when you look at your cape?
* When would you want to wear your confidence cape? In what situations could it help you?
* How will you feel when you wear it as you face challenges?

SUPERHERO SAGA

Turn your child into a superhero! Making a comic book together will help your child see themselves as the superhero of their own story, giving them a confidence boost and highlighting their strengths. Recognizing their superpowers will encourage kids to see themselves in a more confident and loving way.

Age Range:	**5–9**
Skills:	**Creativity, self-reflection**
Materials:	**Paper, pencil, coloring utensils**
Number of Participants:	**1+**
Where to Play:	**Inside or outside**

BEFORE YOU START

* Talk about your child's unique skills and special qualities. Talk about how these can be superpowers in different situations. For example:
  * The power to think positively can help you keep your mind focused on the good of a situation when things feel hard.
  * The power to bounce back from challenges can help you persevere.
* Talk about how superheroes use their special skills for good. Ask your child: "If you were a superhero, how would you face a challenge in your life?"

HOW TO PLAY

* On a blank piece of paper or two, draw rectangles or squares to create a comic book layout. (You can also find printable templates online.)
* Help your child create a superhero that represents them. They can give their superhero a fun name and choose their superpowers. Here are a few examples:
  * Super Shonda, with the power to bounce back when things go wrong
  * The Amazing Amir, with the power to think positively

* Let your child create a short comic about themselves as a superhero overcoming a challenge. Younger children will need more support in creating their story, but older children can do this independently.
* Read the story together as a family.

THINKING BACK AND LOOKING AHEAD

* What is it like to imagine yourself as a superhero?
* How will the special powers and skills you identified help you in real life?
* How can you be the superhero of your own life?

WHAT I LOVE ABOUT YOU

When kids are learning to love themselves, it's helpful to hear what others love about them too! Taking in others' loving views of us helps boost self-confidence and shape the ways we love ourselves. In this activity, you'll let each other know what specific things you love about each other.

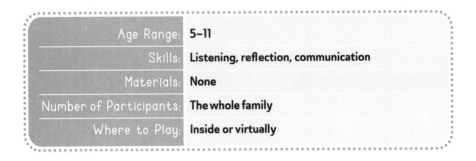

Age Range:	5–11
Skills:	Listening, reflection, communication
Materials:	None
Number of Participants:	The whole family
Where to Play:	Inside or virtually

BEFORE YOU START
★ Talk about how people can express love to others, such as:
- We can say, "I love you!"
- We can say what we love about other people, like the nice things they do, the great qualities they have, or things we appreciate about them.

HOW TO PLAY
★ Take turns highlighting one family member. Each other family member will say, "What I love about you is..." and complete the sentence.
★ Continue until everyone has been highlighted and gotten to hear what others love about them.

THINKING BACK AND LOOKING AHEAD
★ How did it feel to tell someone what you love about them?
★ How did it feel to hear what others love about you?
★ Which thing that someone said was most meaningful to you?
★ How do you think telling each other what we love about each other could make our family better?
★ How would it change your life if we told you what we love about you more often?

CATCH A COMPLIMENT

Keep your eye on the ball (and your heart open)! In this activity, you'll offer compliments to one another to remind everyone of all the awesome things about them. Hearing genuine compliments from others helps kids develop appreciation and love for their unique and special qualities.

Age Range:	**5–11**
Skills:	**Turn taking, listening, communication**
Materials:	**Ball**
Number of Participants:	**3+**
Where to Play:	**Outside**

BEFORE YOU START

★ Talk about what a compliment is and how to give a genuine compliment. You can say something like, "A compliment is something that we say to someone to let them know we like their work or their efforts. Genuine compliments are true and are generally about something other than someone's appearance." Here are some examples:
  - I like all the details you added to your painting.
  - I like how you always include me when you play.
  - I like how you didn't give up when you were learning to do a cartwheel.

HOW TO PLAY

★ Stand in a circle. One person will toss the ball to someone else in the circle. The person who tossed the ball will compliment the person who catches the ball.
★ Continue until everyone has received several compliments.

THINKING BACK AND LOOKING AHEAD

★ How did it feel to get a compliment from someone?
★ How did it feel to give a compliment to someone?
★ What was one compliment that meant a lot to you? Why did it mean a lot to you? How will it stick with you?

MISTAKE MAGIC

The magic in a mistake is that there is always something to learn! Take time to analyze a mistake and make a plan for future improvement to give kids confidence to make positive changes. When they believe they can have positive outcomes in the future, they will feel more confident, less afraid of failing, and more loving toward themselves.

Age Range:	5–11
Skills:	Self-reflection, problem-solving
Materials:	None
Number of Participants:	1+
Where to Play:	Inside or virtually

BEFORE YOU START

★ Remind kids that everyone makes mistakes, and that's okay! Each mistake can teach us something and help us know what to do differently in the future.

HOW TO PLAY

★ When your child makes a mistake, take time to explore some mistake magic.
★ Talk about the mistake. Ask your child these questions:
  • What were the details of the event?
  • What feelings did you have in the moment?
  • What thoughts did you have in the moment?
  • If you could do it over again, what would you do differently?
  • What did you learn from this mistake?
★ Make a plan for the future! Help your child complete these thoughts:
  • When I face a similar problem, I will...
  • I will tell myself...
  • I will ask ____ for help.
  • When I face a similar problem in the future, I will feel...

THINKING BACK AND LOOKING AHEAD

★ What was it like to think about a mistake like this?

★ How are you feeling about the mistake now?

★ How comfortable do you feel talking about mistakes, on a scale of 0–10? (0= not at all comfortable, 10 = completely comfortable)

Head to your library and look for these awesome children's books about making mistakes:

- *Beautiful Oops!* by Barney Saltzberg

- *The Most Magnificent Thing* by Ashley Spires

- *The Girl Who Never Made Mistakes* by Mark Pett and Gary Rubinstein

- *Mistakes That Worked* by Charlotte Foltz Jones, illustrated by John O'Brien

SCAVENGER HUNT

Grab a clipboard and set out for adventure! Going on a scavenger hunt encourages problem-solving and gives kids a sense of accomplishment as they check things off their lists. That sense of accomplishment and confidence will help kids feel good about themselves and their efforts.

Age Range:	**5–11**
Skills:	**Problem-solving, perseverance**
Materials:	**Clipboards, paper, pencils**
Number of Participants:	**1+**
Where to Play:	**Inside or outside**

BEFORE YOU START

* Make a list of age-appropriate items for kids to find. Give younger kids easier options and older children more advanced items. Older kids might enjoy clues that are riddles, such as "This item gets wet as it dries" for a towel.
* If you're staying inside, items could be things like:
  * A blue sock
  * A picture of the whole family
  * A book that makes you laugh
* If you're heading outside, items could be things like:
  * A green leaf
  * A ladybug or butterfly
  * A cute pet
* If you have a lot of children playing, you could consider making small teams.

HOW TO PLAY

* Give kids clipboards with paper listing their scavenger hunt challenge items.
* As kids find items from the scavenger hunt, they can cross them off the list.
* When they find everything on the list or time is up, find a small way to celebrate.

THINKING BACK AND LOOKING AHEAD

* How did you feel when you found items on your list?
* Which item was hardest to find? How did you feel when it was hard to find? How did you feel when you finally found it?
* Were there any items that you had to use creativity to find?
* How did it feel if you were able to complete the whole list?

ADVENTURE DAY

In this activity, you'll work with your child to choose something adventurous to try. Stepping a little out of their comfort zone will help your child try new things, enjoy success, and build confidence—all of which lead to higher self-esteem and self-love.

Age Range:	**5–11**
Skills:	**Flexibility**
Materials:	**Situationally dependent**
Number of Participants:	**1+**
Where to Play:	**Inside or outside**

BEFORE YOU START

★ Talk about what it means to be adventurous. You might say something like, "Being adventurous means that we try new things that might feel a little bit scary, but we face the challenge and find the fun in it."
★ Talk about times when your child has tried something outside their comfort zone in the past. Remind them how they felt when they tried something new.

HOW TO PLAY

★ Together with your child, choose something adventurous to do. Pick something that is a bit outside your child's comfort zone but not too scary.
★ Some indoor adventures could include:
  • Building a fort
  • Writing and performing a play
  • Doing a family talent show
★ Some outdoor adventures could include:
  • Going for a hike
  • Trying a new sport
  • Climbing a rock wall

* Face the adventure together, offering encouragement to your child along the way. Remind them of times that they've stepped outside their comfort zone successfully before.

THINKING BACK AND LOOKING AHEAD

* How did you feel while trying a new adventure?
* Were there times when you felt like you couldn't do it? How did you get past that?
* What other adventures or challenges would you like to try in the future?

YOU'VE GOT MAIL

Sometimes, we all need a little note of encouragement! Make your own mailboxes so you can deliver confidence-boosting mail to one another. Reading loving words from others will help kids develop loving words and thoughts about themselves.

Age Range:	**5–11**
Skills:	**Creativity, communication**
Materials:	**Shoeboxes, cardboard shipping boxes, or plastic bins; construction paper; glue; markers; stickers**
Number of Participants:	**2+**
Where to Play:	**Inside**

BEFORE YOU START

★ Talk about what it means to offer words of encouragement. Say something like, "Words of encouragement are things we can say to help others feel confident and brave." These questions can prompt kids to think of encouraging words:
  • What words make you feel good?
  • What can people say to help you feel like you can do hard things or face challenges?
  • What can you say to others to encourage them?

HOW TO PLAY

★ Give children materials to make their own mailboxes. You can use any supplies you have on hand, like shoeboxes, cardboard shipping boxes, or plastic bins. Decorate the mailboxes with construction paper, markers, stickers, or anything else you want to use!
★ Decide on a place where each mailbox can be placed. This could be by the children's bedroom doors, at the feet of their beds, or somewhere else in the home. You could also do this in a school or group setting.
★ Challenge everyone to write notes of encouragement to put in others' mailboxes.

THINKING BACK AND LOOKING AHEAD

* How does it feel to find encouraging notes in your mailbox?
* How does it feel to know others believe in you?
* How will the notes of encouragement stick with you?

ROLLING PRAISE

Offering praise and compliments to everyone in a group will remind participants of their amazing qualities and all the great things they do. Hearing the good things others appreciate and notice helps kids develop love for themselves as well.

Age Range:	**6–11**
Skills:	**Turn taking, listening, communication**
Materials:	**1 game die**
Number of Participants:	**3+**
Where to Play:	**Inside or outside**

BEFORE YOU START

★ Review what a compliment is and how to give genuine praise. We can offer compliments or praise to someone about:
- Their performance on something
- Their effort on something
- The way they treat others
- A great quality they have
- Something awesome they did

HOW TO PLAY

★ Choose one person to receive praise first.
★ Roll the game die. The rest of the group will give the person who is receiving praise the same number of compliments as the number on the die. So, if a 4 is rolled, the recipient will get four compliments from each person.
★ Continue until everyone has had at least one turn.

THINKING BACK AND LOOKING AHEAD

★ How did it feel to get a compliment from someone?
★ How did it feel to give a compliment to someone?
★ What was one compliment that meant a lot to you? Why did it mean a lot to you? How will it stick with you?

IF I HAD NO FEAR, I WOULD...

This activity encourages kids to push the limits of their imaginations to see themselves as powerful and brave. Helping kids imagine what they would do without fear can give them a confidence boost and a chance to imagine themselves in new situations. Recognizing that fear is a normal emotion and thinking about things they'd like to do despite it will help kids feel more loving and gentle toward themselves.

Age Range:	**7–11**
Skills:	**Self-reflection, communication**
Materials:	**Paper, drawing utensils (optional)**
Number of Participants:	**1+**
Where to Play:	**Inside or virtually**

BEFORE YOU START

★ Talk about what fear is and how it affects us. You might say something like, "Fear is a feeling we can have when we face something scary, new, or challenging. Fear can make it hard to think or cause us to hold back and not give things our all. It can also make us change the way we act or the way we show ourselves to others."

HOW TO PLAY

★ Challenge your child to complete the sentence "If I had no fear, I would..." This can be a general prompt, or you can apply it to a specific situation, like moving to a new school, joining a sports team, or something else your child is facing.

★ You can simply make this a conversation or turn it into an art activity! Kids can verbally share their response to this prompt or draw a picture to show what they would do if they had no fear.

THINKING BACK AND LOOKING AHEAD

★ What is it like to think about not having fear?
★ Where do you think your fear comes from?
★ What steps could we take together to help you feel less fear?
★ What would it feel like to take these next steps?

ACT IT OUT

A little practice can go a long way to building confidence! To give kids a confidence boost before they officially try something new, approach a challenge, or attempt to attain a goal, try role-playing at home. Practicing their actions and words will help them feel more confident when they face the real situation.

Age Range:	8–11
Skills:	Self-reflection
Materials:	None
Number of Participants:	1+
Where to Play:	Inside or virtually

BEFORE YOU START

* Talk about a challenge that is upcoming for your child. Remind them that it's okay to feel a little bit nervous when we don't know what to expect. Explain that acting it out can help them feel more confident when they are really in the situation.

HOW TO PLAY

* Role-play the upcoming challenge. This is especially helpful if the challenge involves a conflict with another person or if your child needs to ask for help or advocate for their own needs when you aren't around (like at school). If you want, you can play your child while they play another person involved. Demonstrate positive self-talk or self-advocacy that your child could use in the moment. For example, you might say:
  * Can we please talk about what happened yesterday? I felt sad, and I hoped we could talk about what would be better in the future.
  * I am really confused. Can you help me, please?
  * This is hard. I made a mistake. I'll try a new strategy.
* Then switch roles so your child can practice as themselves after seeing you model this for them.

THINKING BACK AND LOOKING AHEAD

* How did it feel to practice?
* What was it like to see me act it out as you? Did I say or do anything that you think would be helpful for you to do?
* How are you feeling about facing this challenge now that we've practiced?

VISUALIZE SUCCESS

If you can dream it, you can do it! Kids will take a moment to visualize success in an upcoming activity or challenge. Picturing themselves succeeding can help kids feel more confident, and more confidence creates self-love.

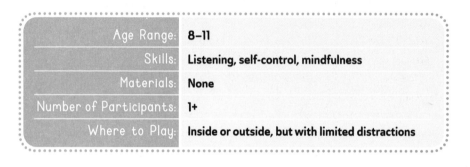

Age Range:	**8–11**
Skills:	**Listening, self-control, mindfulness**
Materials:	**None**
Number of Participants:	**1+**
Where to Play:	**Inside or outside, but with limited distractions**

BEFORE YOU START

★ Explain what visualization is. You could say something like, "Visualization is when we picture something in our minds. Visualizing ourselves doing things, overcoming challenges, or working toward our goals can help us feel more confident to do those things in real life!"

HOW TO PLAY

★ Sit comfortably in a place with limited distractions.
★ Read the following script to your child:

Sit comfortably in your space. If you would like to, you can close your eyes for this activity. If you are not comfortable closing your eyes, that's okay too. You may want to find a spot or image that you would like to focus your eyes on as you listen to my voice during this activity.

In your mind, think of something you want to accomplish, a challenge that's coming up, or a goal you want to achieve. Just take a moment to think about the challenge or goal.

Notice the feeling you have as you think about this situation.

Now think of someone you know who has been through something similar. It can be a real person you know or maybe a book character or someone from TV or a movie. How did that person overcome the situation? What steps did they take to overcome the challenge or reach their goal?

Shift your attention back to yourself. Imagine yourself taking those same steps to overcome your challenge or reach your goal. Are there other steps you think might help? Imagine yourself following through with those steps that would help you deal with the problem or achieve the goal. Picture it in your mind.

As you imagine yourself overcoming the challenge, do you picture any specific people around you? Are there people helping you through this?

Notice how it feels as you imagine yourself overcoming the challenge or reaching the goal. What emotions do you have?

THINKING BACK AND LOOKING AHEAD

* How did you feel while you pictured yourself facing the challenge or reaching your goal?
* What steps did you picture?
* On a scale of 1–10, how confident are you when you think about facing that challenge or reaching that goal? How can I help you feel more confident?

GOAL LADDER

Time to climb the ladder of success! Setting a goal for the future can help kids build confidence for approaching new tasks. Confident kids are more loving toward themselves.

Age Range:	**9–11**
Skills:	**Self-reflection, problem-solving, perseverance**
Materials:	**Paper, pencil**
Number of Participants:	**1+**
Where to Play:	**Inside or outside**

BEFORE YOU START

★ Talk about goals that your child has. Let them choose one goal that is really meaningful to them.

★ Remind them that when we work toward goals, it's okay to make small progress along the way—we might not achieve the full goal right away. Small steps are progress, and progress is important.

HOW TO PLAY

★ On a piece of paper, draw a ladder. At the top of the ladder, write a goal the child is working toward. At the bottom of the ladder, write what they can do right now relating to the goal.

★ On the steps in between, have the child write what small progress toward the goal would look like. Here's an example:
  • Bottom of ladder: I am in drama class at school.
  • Step 1: Practice skits at home with my sister.
  • Step 2: Practice the songs from the play.
  • Step 3: Memorize the lines for the part I want.
  • Step 4: Try out for the play.
  • Top of ladder: Get a role in the school play.

THINKING BACK AND LOOKING AHEAD

★ How does it feel to see the small steps you can take to work toward it?

★ How will you feel when you reach each step on the ladder?

★ How will you feel when you achieve your goal?

CHAPTER 5

COMPETENCE

WHAT IS COMPETENCE?

Competence is a kid's ability to do things with success or with efficiency—in other words, a child who is competent can do something well. Competence is different from confidence in a key way: Confidence is the *belief* that you can do something, while competence is actually being able to do it. Both are necessary components of self-love!

HOW DOES COMPETENCE RELATE TO SELF-LOVE?

When children are successful, they feel satisfied and proud. People who are competent, or have the skills, characteristics, or qualities to accomplish a task, are more likely to be successful. Therefore, competence is related to feelings of pride and satisfaction, both of which promote self-love. When kids feel good about their abilities and the outcomes they achieve with those abilities, they feel good about themselves too.

If kids develop competence in a variety of areas, they are better able to approach new tasks, new situations, challenges, and roadblocks with the mindset that they will have positive outcomes and love themselves anyway even when more challenges arise.

WHAT DOES COMPETENCE LOOK AND SOUND LIKE?

The outward demonstration of competence involves completing tasks with efficiency and success. Some examples of outward demonstrations of competence include:

★ Completing tasks or assignments
★ Meeting expectations
★ Reaching for goals and honoring progress made

COMPETENCE IN KID-FRIENDLY TERMS

To explain competence to your kid, try saying something like this:

There are going to be so many new things for you to try as you grow and learn. Some things will be hard at first, but as you keep trying and practice, you'll notice that you get better! When you can do things on your own and do them well, that's called competence. Being competent means you can get the job done or complete the task. You can develop competence by trying to solve problems, trying new strategies, learning new ways of doing things, and persevering even when things get hard.

LOOKING AHEAD

In this chapter, you'll find activities that encourage kids to try things on their own, problem-solve, and identify things they do well. You'll also find activities that help kids work toward goals, monitor their progress, and celebrate efforts and progress along the way.

TRUSTY ASSISTANT

Everyone needs a little help sometimes, even adults! Kids can be great assistants, and feeling like they are contributing and helping an adult in some way helps kids feel a sense of competence that they can apply to other areas of their lives.

Age Range:	**5–7**
Skills:	**Cooperation, communication**
Materials:	**Situationally dependent**
Number of Participants:	**1+**
Where to Play:	**Inside or outside**

BEFORE YOU START

* Identify a task or job that is typically something just adults handle but is also appropriate for kids to help with. This should be something outside of the child's regular chores or expectations.
* Be sure to choose a task or project that is low stakes and not emotionally charged. The goal of this activity is to give kids an opportunity to help, feel like they are contributing, and develop a sense of competence in the role they are given. This isn't the time to let the five-year-old help with an oil change!
* Some examples of tasks kids can help with are:
  * Making a grocery list
  * Shopping for groceries
  * Organizing a toolbox or tackle box
  * Sorting the laundry

HOW TO PLAY

* When you have a task or project, invite your trusty assistant to help you.
* Give them a special role or job in the project. Make sure they know you *really* need their help and that you're depending on them to get the task done.

(continued on next page)

* Give the kid simple instructions for helping, and be sure to offer lots of reinforcement and praise along the way. This could sound like:
  * Wow, that was really helpful! Thanks!
  * You did that exactly like I needed you to. Thanks for listening to my instructions.
  * Wow! You really are a great helper. I'm glad you're my assistant today.

THINKING BACK AND LOOKING AHEAD

* How did it feel to be my assistant today?
* Were there any other parts of the job that you think you could have also helped with?
* What other tasks might you like to be my assistant for?

CATERPILLAR, BUTTERFLY

Every caterpillar earns its wings...with time! Celebrate what your child is able to do right now, and help them see what they will be able to do in the future with practice and effort. Seeing how their current abilities will turn into their future abilities will help kids feel competent, confident, and eager to try new things.

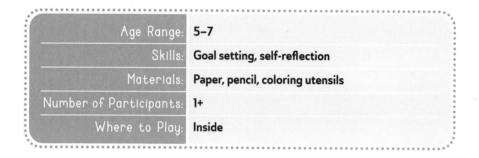

Age Range:	**5–7**
Skills:	**Goal setting, self-reflection**
Materials:	**Paper, pencil, coloring utensils**
Number of Participants:	**1+**
Where to Play:	**Inside**

BEFORE YOU START

★ Talk about how caterpillars are baby butterflies. At first, caterpillars can only inch their way around the world. As they grow and mature over time, eventually, they can fly! They gain a whole new view and perspective of the world. Find a video online that shows the transformation from caterpillar to butterfly to help your child create a mental picture of the process.

★ Explain to your child that right now, they might feel like a caterpillar. They might be able to do something small, but they may not yet be able to do something big they really want to do. As they grow, mature, and practice, just like a butterfly, they will be able to do something amazing!

HOW TO PLAY

★ Turn the paper horizontally. On the left side, draw a caterpillar at the top of the page. On the right side, draw a butterfly at the top of the page.

★ Have your child draw a picture of something they can do on the caterpillar side.

★ Have your child draw a picture of something they will be able to do with a little more practice on the butterfly side.

(continued on next page)

THINKING BACK AND LOOKING AHEAD

* ★ How does it feel to be like a caterpillar?
* ★ How will you feel when you are like a butterfly?
* ★ Who can help you be like a butterfly and learn how to do that big thing you want to be able to do?

WEEKLY WINS

What was your child's win this week? Take time to celebrate small victories, progress over perfection, hard work, and good experiences from the week to help kids feel a sense of growth and competence. Celebrating even the smallest victories will help kids recognize their own improvements and develop a more optimistic view of themselves and the world.

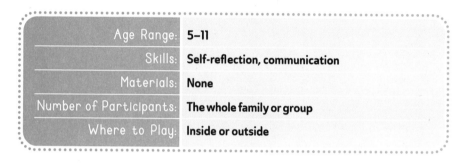

Age Range:	**5–11**
Skills:	**Self-reflection, communication**
Materials:	**None**
Number of Participants:	**The whole family or group**
Where to Play:	**Inside or outside**

BEFORE YOU START

* ★ Designate a special day and time during the week to do this activity regularly.
* ★ Try your best to make this a routine. Doing it regularly will help kids feel a sense of competence when they take time to reflect on their progress or successes.

HOW TO PLAY

* ★ Sit together in a circle on the floor, at a table, or gathered around the living room.
* ★ Everyone will take turns sharing their "weekly wins." A weekly win is something that went well during the week. It can be small progress toward a goal, an achievement, or simply something good that happened. Use this time to encourage kids to recognize their own efforts; small, good details of the week; or successes. Weekly wins could include things like:
  * I finished my science project!
  * I improved my math score from last week.
  * I made more free throws in my game this week than last week.
  * I made a new friend.
  * I worked out a problem with a friend.
* ★ Continue until everyone has had a chance to share.

(continued on next page)

THINKING BACK AND LOOKING AHEAD

* What was it like to think about your wins this week?
* How did it feel to share them with others?
* How does it feel to compare your wins this week to your wins last week?
* Where do you hope to be next week?

SUCCESS WALL

Visual reminders of success can help encourage kids to try new things, take risks, and remember their past efforts. Create a success wall in your home to celebrate all those things! Seeing what they're doing well will help kids feel good about their efforts and successes and feel positively about themselves.

Age Range:	**5–11**
Skills:	**Self-reflection**
Materials:	**Display space, such as a wall, refrigerator, frame, or poster board; tape or hanging hardware**
Number of Participants:	**The whole family**
Where to Play:	**Inside**

BEFORE YOU START

★ Talk about what it means to be successful. You can say something like, "Success does not mean we always get it right on the first try. Success might mean that we make progress or that we have small improvements toward a goal."

★ Discuss how success also doesn't have to be an achievement or an award. It can be showing kindness to others. It can be including others. It can be showing generosity to the community. Talk about how you want to define success for your family.

HOW TO PLAY

★ Designate a specific space for a success wall. This could be on an actual wall, on the refrigerator, or on a poster board that is movable.

★ Display visual reminders of success. These could include things like:
  • An improved grade on a test
  • An art project
  • An award ribbon
  • A picture of your child crossing a finish line
  • A thank-you note from someone who appreciated a family member

(continued on next page)

* Each time something is added to the success wall, bring the group together to celebrate!

THINKING BACK AND LOOKING AHEAD

* How does it feel to add something to the success wall?
* How does it feel to see your successes displayed?
* How does it feel to celebrate your success with the whole family?
* Now that you see this success on the wall, what else might you like to work toward?

EXPERT INTERVIEW

Calling all experts! Gather around for a panel of the minds. Let your child choose something they are an expert in. Ask them questions and let their expertise shine. Acting as an expert who can share their knowledge with others will help kids feel good about themselves, knowing they are competent and capable of awesome things.

Age Range:	**5–11**
Skills:	**Communication, public speaking**
Materials:	**Visuals like pictures, books, stuffed animals, building models, or anything else to support your child's expert moment (optional)**
Number of Participants:	**The whole family or group**
Where to Play:	**Inside or outside**

BEFORE YOU START

* Talk about what it means to be an expert. You could say something like, "An expert is someone who knows *a lot* about something. They can answer other people's questions about the topic and help other people learn about it too. Experts don't have to be adults—kids can know a lot about topics too!"

HOW TO PLAY

* Let your child choose something they feel like an expert in. This can be anything! They could be an expert on dinosaurs, building Lego models, drawing cats, doing ballet, doing a backward roll, *PAW Patrol*, or any other topic they are passionate about.
* Set a time for your expert interview, during which your child will present their topic to the family or group. If they want to simply talk about the topic, that's fine! They can also share books, show pictures they have drawn, or do a demonstration to help others understand the topic.

(continued on next page)

★ After they have shared about the topic, audience members should interview the expert by asking follow-up questions about the topic. Everyone should listen intently as they highlight their expertise.

★ Let everyone in the group thank the expert for their time and for sharing their knowledge.

THINKING BACK AND LOOKING AHEAD

★ How did it feel to be the expert?

★ What was it like to share everything you know about this topic with the family or group?

★ What other topics might you want to share with us?

★ What else do you want to learn about this topic now?

★ Are there any other topics you want to learn about now?

CAN-DO ALPHABET

Sometimes, kids don't even realize all the amazing things they can do, especially if they compare themselves to older siblings or adults. Exercise creativity while emphasizing competence by making a list of all the things kids can do from A to Z. This will help them celebrate things they can do and see themselves with love.

Age Range:	**5–11**
Skills:	**Self-reflection, creativity**
Materials:	**Paper, pencil, coloring utensils, or sidewalk chalk; frame (optional)**
Number of Participants:	**1+**
Where to Play:	**Inside or outside**

BEFORE YOU START
★ Talk about all the things your child can do. Ask them to think of things they can do at home, at school, with friends, outside, while helping out at home, and so on.

HOW TO PLAY
★ On paper or on the sidewalk, write letters from A to Z.
★ For each letter, help your child identify something they can do that starts with that letter. Older kids can write their own list, but younger kids might need assistance. For example:
  • A: act in a play
  • B: build a fort
  • C: cartwheel
★ If you make the list on paper, you may want to let your child draw a picture or a symbol to represent each thing they came up with for each letter. Hang it somewhere that your child will see it often, or frame it.
★ If you make the list on the sidewalk, take a picture of your child beside the list and display the photo in your home so your child can remember all the amazing things they can do!

(continued on next page)

* Repeat this activity once a year to compare the incredible things your kid can do as they grow.

THINKING BACK AND LOOKING AHEAD

* What is it like to see this list of all the things you can do?
* Were you surprised by all the things we came up with? Why or why not?
* How does it feel to know you can do all these things?

....

For difficult letters like Q or X. encourage your child to be creative! They might come up with something like "quickly clean up my room" for Q or "eXcite others" for X.

....

WHAT WOULD YOU DO?

Thinking about possible situations, mulling over options, and deciding on actions gives kids a sense of confidence and competence to handle challenges that might come up later. Pose some questions over dinner or on a car ride to give your kid a chance to think and talk through the options. As they feel more confident to handle a variety of situations, kids will be better equipped to take on the world with a loving attitude toward themselves.

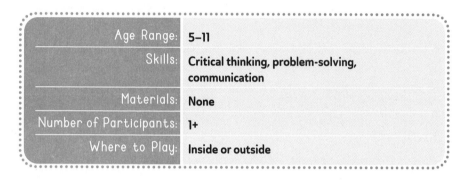

Age Range:	**5–11**
Skills:	**Critical thinking, problem-solving, communication**
Materials:	**None**
Number of Participants:	**1+**
Where to Play:	**Inside or outside**

BEFORE YOU START

★ Talk about what it looks like to think through your options in a situation.
  • First, identify the problem.
  • Second, think of at least two possible ways to handle the problem.
  • Next, think about the possible outcomes or consequences of those choices.
  • Finally, decide which choice is the best one.

HOW TO PLAY

★ While you're sitting down for dinner, waiting in line together at the pharmacy, or on a long car ride, pose questions to your kid to find out how they would handle situations. Here are some sample situations:

(continued on next page)

Age	Situations
4–5	⋆ Your sibling has a toy that you really want to play with. They walk away to go to the bathroom and leave the toy behind. What would you do?
	⋆ Your aunt makes cookies for the neighbors. You really want one, but she told you not to touch the cookies. She leaves them on the counter to cool and goes upstairs to talk on the phone. What would you do?
	⋆ You are playing by yourself in the living room. You throw a ball, and it knocks over a lamp and breaks it. No one sees it happen. What would you do?
6–8	⋆ You are playing with your friends at recess at school. A girl who's new to your school is sitting by herself. You don't want to leave your friends, but she looks lonely. What would you do?
	⋆ You and your sibling are playing inside and make a really big mess. You go to another room to play, and you hear your dad scolding your sibling for making the mess, but he doesn't say anything to you. What would you do?
9–11	⋆ Some kids at school are teasing a boy in your class. He looks sad, but you don't want them to tease you too. What would you do?
	⋆ Your friend invites you over to play. You really want to go, but you know the rule is that you have to do your homework first, and you haven't started. Your mom asks if you have homework today. What would you do?

⋆ Give them a chance to think through their options, talk about possible outcomes and consequences, and decide on the best course of action. For younger children, you can offer support as they work through these steps. Help them first identify the problem, then think of solutions, and so forth. Older children may be able to do this without support after a few times practicing.

⋆ Share what you would do as well to offer a different perspective.

THINKING BACK AND LOOKING AHEAD

⋆ How does it feel to think about your choices?

⋆ Is it easy or hard to think about what might happen?

⋆ How confident are you to handle situations like these?

DECISION TREE

Tall trees grow from strong roots! This activity will use a tree visual to help kids make decisions about a variety of things. When kids feel like they have competent decision-making skills, they feel better about themselves, which will help them flourish with self-love!

Age Range:	6–11
Skills:	Decision-making, critical thinking, problem-solving, planning
Materials:	Paper, pencil
Number of Participants:	1+
Where to Play:	Inside

BEFORE YOU START

★ Talk about how we always have choices when confronting any problem. We can choose the words we say, the actions we decide to take, and the way we treat others.
★ Talk about what it looks like to think through your options in a situation.
  • First, identify the problem.
  • Second, think of all the ways you could choose to handle the problem.
  • Next, think about the possible outcomes or consequences of those choices.
  • Finally, decide which choice is the best one.

HOW TO PLAY

★ Turn the paper vertically. Draw a tree trunk on the paper.
★ On the tree trunk, write a situation or problem that your child is trying to make a decision about. It could be something like:
  • Should I try out for soccer or baseball?
  • Should I invite just one friend to do something big with me for my birthday or several friends to do something small?
  • What should I do if I have a disagreement with my friend?

(continued on next page)

* Talk about all the choices your child has in the situation. For each decision, draw one branch on the tree trunk. Write the choices on the branches.
* For each choice, talk about the possible outcomes or consequences. Draw a leaf on the branch for each possible outcome or consequence, and write the outcomes or consequences inside the leaves.
* After evaluating all the choices and possible outcomes, help your child choose the best option. Draw an apple on the branch of the choice that they pick!

THINKING BACK AND LOOKING AHEAD
* What was it like to think through all your options?
* What was it like to imagine the possible outcomes or consequences?
* How do you feel when you look at your decision tree?
* How does this process help you feel confident to face the problem?

MARBLE RUN BOARD

In this creative STEM challenge, kids will learn by trial and error. Making mistakes, brainstorming small corrections, and seeing their efforts pay off will help kids develop a sense of mastery that leaves them feeling great. This competence helps kids feel proud of themselves.

Age Range:	**7–11**
Skills:	**Planning, problem-solving, perseverance**
Materials:	**Cardboard, painter's tape, empty toilet paper or paper towel rolls, plastic cup, 1 marble, a variety of other craft supplies**
Number of Participants:	**1+**
Where to Play:	**Inside or outside**

BEFORE YOU START

★ Talk about how sometimes when we try to solve a problem, it doesn't work out the first time. We have to make small changes, try new strategies, and look at problems from different angles to be able to solve them.

★ Share with your child about a time when you needed to solve a problem or built something and it didn't work perfectly the first time. Tell them about small changes you made, how you felt when things didn't work, how you felt when you tried again, and how you felt when it finally worked.

★ Talk about some strategies they can use when they experience frustration at things not working out the first time. They can:
  - Take slow, deep breaths.
  - Think about a similar problem they solved before.
  - Try a different strategy.
  - Speak positively to themselves (I can do this!).
  - Ask for help.

(continued on next page)

HOW TO PLAY

* Tape a large piece of cardboard to the wall.
* On the top-left area of the cardboard, attach an empty toilet paper roll with the tape.
* On the bottom-right area of the cardboard, attach the plastic cup.
* Challenge your child to build a marble run that can get a marble from the top-left toilet paper roll to the cup at the bottom.
* Kids can tape items like other paper towel rolls to the cardboard to make a path for the marble using painter's tape, which is easily peeled off and reattached when they need to make small corrections.
* Let kids be creative with their paths. Younger kids will need adult support, but older kids can do this independently. If you are supporting your child while they create the path, offer encouragement and feedback with statements like:
  * That was a cool idea! It didn't quite work. What small change could you make and then try again?
  * This part worked so well! It seemed to get stuck in this part. How do you think you could change this part to make it work as well as the first part?
* When they create a successful marble path, celebrate their success!

THINKING BACK AND LOOKING AHEAD

* How did it feel when the marble fell out of the path?
* What small changes did you make?
* How did it feel when a small change made a big difference?
* How did you feel when you finally made a successful path?
* What other things do you think you could use these problem-solving strategies for?

I CAN, I WILL

There's always room for growth! Celebrate and recognize what your child can do right now while still keeping a focus on how they want to grow in the future. Highlighting competence and areas of growth will encourage kids to keep moving forward and help them feel good not only about where they are but where they will end up! Evaluating how they are successful and how they can improve can remind kids to be loving toward themselves as they continue to grow.

Age Range:	**8–11**
Skills:	**Goal setting, planning, self-reflection**
Materials:	**Poster board or paper, markers**
Number of Participants:	**1+**
Where to Play:	**Inside**

BEFORE YOU START

★ Talk about growth. You might say, "We all have things we can do right now. We all have things we want to be able to do in the future. The things we can do now can help us achieve the things we want to be able to do in the future."

★ Share stories with your child about things you wanted to learn how to do. Tell them about the feelings you had, what motivated you to move forward, and how you got there.

HOW TO PLAY

★ Turn the poster board or paper horizontally. Draw a vertical line down the middle to divide the paper into two equal sections.

★ On the left side, write "I Can." On the right side, write "I Will."

★ On the left side, have your child write or draw pictures of things they can do right now. They might include things like:
  • A cartwheel
  • Write my name
  • Draw a fish
  • Make a peanut butter and jelly sandwich

(continued on next page)

* On the right side, have your child write or draw pictures of things they believe they will be able to do in the future. They might include things like:
  * Do a front handspring
  * Write my name in cursive
  * Draw a turtle in the ocean
  * Make a grilled cheese sandwich
* Talk about the differences in the two lists.
  * Are there any things on the left side that can help them achieve the things on the right side?
  * What strategies do they know of that can help them learn to do the things on the right side?
  * Are there any people who could help them learn how to do the things on the right side?
* Hang the poster or paper somewhere visible in the home, like on the refrigerator or on a bulletin board. Reference it often, and encourage your kid to move things from the right side to the left as they learn how to do them and master the skills!

THINKING BACK AND LOOKING AHEAD

* How does it feel to identify things you can already do? Can you remember a time when you weren't able to do those things? How does it feel now that you can do them?
* How do you feel when you look at the things you can't do yet but will be able to?
* How do you think you will feel when you can do those things?

PLANNING PETALS

In this activity, kids will create a beautiful visual representation to encourage planning and progress toward a goal. Mapping out the steps to work toward a goal can help keep kids focused, on track, and motivated to continue moving forward, all while helping them feel good about the work they're putting into their goal. Setting, working toward, and achieving goals will help kids develop senses of competency and confidence, both of which contribute to self-love.

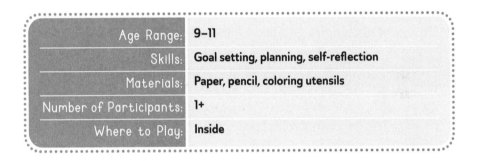

Age Range:	**9–11**
Skills:	**Goal setting, planning, self-reflection**
Materials:	**Paper, pencil, coloring utensils**
Number of Participants:	**1+**
Where to Play:	**Inside**

BEFORE YOU START

★ Think about how you can help your child reach their goal. For example, after planning the steps toward your child's goal, imagine how you'll talk about some potential roadblocks. Some questions to consider:
  - What might get in the way of making progress on the goal?
  - How can you (or we) address these roadblocks if they come up?
  - How might it feel to face a challenge or roadblock when you're working toward your goal?
  - Who are some people who can help you if you face a challenge or roadblock?
★ Consider whether you want to have your child draw a "thorn" on the stem of the goal flower each time a roadblock or challenge comes up. These will serve as a visual reminder of the challenges they overcame after they achieve their goal.

(continued on next page)

HOW TO PLAY

* Together, talk about a goal that your child has or something they would like to accomplish. Make a list of all the necessary steps to accomplish the goal. For example, if your child wants to write their own book, the steps might be:
    * Brainstorm ideas for the book.
    * Write a first draft.
    * Edit the first draft and write a final draft.
    * Create the illustrations.
    * Combine the text and illustrations.
    * Draw a cover.
    * Put all the pages and cover together.
* On a piece of paper, draw a circle in the center. Have your child write their goal in the circle.
* Around the circle, draw a petal for each step you identified to achieve the goal (for the previous example, you would draw seven petals around the circle). In each petal, write a step toward the goal.
* As your child completes steps toward the goal, they will color in the petals.
* When your child has reached their goal, the whole flower will be colored.
* For extra celebration, cut out completed flowers and display them somewhere special so your child can have a visual reminder of all their hard work and progress.

THINKING BACK AND LOOKING AHEAD

* How are you feeling now that you have reached your goal?
* Which step toward your goal was most difficult?
* What roadblocks did you face? How did you overcome them?
* What did you learn about yourself while you were working toward your goal?
* What new goal do you want to achieve now that you have accomplished this one?

VISUAL PROGRESS

Setting a goal and tracking progress toward that goal helps kids visualize how they're doing and stay motivated to keep moving. As they see their success represented visually, they'll feel more confident, competent, and proud.

Age Range:	9–11
Skills:	Goal setting, planning, self-reflection
Materials:	Paper, pencils, coloring utensils
Number of Participants:	1+
Where to Play:	Inside

BEFORE YOU START

* Talk about what a goal is. You could say something like, "A goal is something that we want to achieve, accomplish, or learn how to do. Sometimes, it takes a long time to reach a goal! We can break a big goal into smaller parts to make it feel more manageable."
* Give kids an example of breaking a big goal into smaller, more manageable goals. Here's an example for younger kids:
  * Big goal: I want my room to be totally clean.
  * Smaller goals:
    * I will put away all my clean clothes.
    * I will put my dirty clothes in the hamper.
    * I will put all my blocks in the block box.
    * I will put all my stuffed animals on my bed.
    * I will make my bed.
    * I will put my towel in the bathroom.
* Here's an example for older kids:
  * Big goal: I want to run a mile in 8 minutes, 30 seconds.
  * Smaller goals:
    * I will walk a mile without stopping.
    * I will run a mile in 10 minutes, walking a bit if I need to.
    * I will run a mile in 9 minutes, 30 seconds.
    * I will run a mile in 9 minutes.
    * I will run a mile in 8 minutes, 30 seconds.

(continued on next page)

* Work with your child to identify their goal. Once the big goal is identified, help your child break the goal into smaller, more manageable parts.
* On the paper, make a visual representation of the small parts. Here are a few examples:
  * Draw a ladder. Include one rung on the ladder for each step toward the goal.
  * For the running goal mentioned previously, draw one tennis shoe for each progress step.
  * If your child's goal is to read one hundred books this year, draw one hundred rectangles on the paper.
* Each time your child completes a step toward their goal, color one step of the visual. This visual representation of the progress made will keep kids motivated and help them see how far they've come.
* Hang the visual somewhere highly visible at home. Reference it often to keep their goal in mind!

THINKING BACK AND LOOKING AHEAD

* How does it feel to see how much progress you've made toward your goal?
* How does it feel to see how much progress you have left toward your goal?
* How will you feel when you reach the end?

CHAPTER 6

PURPOSE AND CONTRIBUTION

WHAT ARE PURPOSE AND CONTRIBUTION?

A sense of purpose helps drive kids toward a desired outcome or **end goal**. When they make a meaningful contribution, kids feel like they're giving **back** and like they are an important part of the group or community.

HOW DO PURPOSE AND CONTRIBUTION RELATE TO SELF-LOVE?

Having a sense of purpose is closely related to an understanding **of your** skills and qualities and the ways they can be used to achieve a **meaningful** goal. When kids are aware of their skills and appreciate their **own qualities** and attributes, they feel better about themselves. Furthermore, **when they** recognize how they can use those skills, qualities, and attributes in meaning-ful ways to connect to those around them, self-love flourishes.

When kids feel like they can contribute to their families, groups, **neighbor-**hoods, communities, and world, self-love is likely to be boosted. Believing they can contribute to the world around them with their unique **and special** qualities is an effective path for kids to develop self-love.

WHAT DO PURPOSE AND CONTRIBUTION LOOK AND SOUND LIKE?

The outward demonstrations of purpose and contribution are **easy to see**. These are the actionable steps that are visible when self-love and **a desire** for connectedness are flowing.

Some examples of outward demonstrations of purpose and contribution include:

* Volunteering
* Standing up for others
* Working toward a long-term goal
* Connecting interests to purpose—for example, if a child who loves animals volunteers at a local animal shelter
* Helping out at home
* Seeking connections with others in the community or neighborhood
* Being passionate about doing good things

PURPOSE AND CONTRIBUTION IN KID-FRIENDLY TERMS

To explain purpose and contribution to your kid, try saying something like this:

> When you feel excited and energized about things in the world, and when you want to go out and make positive changes in the world, you might have found a sense of purpose! "Purpose" means that you have your mind set on achieving something or doing something that feels important to you and gives you a feeling of warmth and makes your heart feel full.
>
> "Contribution" means that you are giving to the people around you. You can give your time, energy, or kind words or actions. All these things contribute to make things better for the people around you.

LOOKING AHEAD

In this chapter, you'll find activities that encourage kids to explore their passions and interests to find that sense of purpose. You'll also find activities that help kids contribute to their family, their neighborhood, and the larger community around them.

YOU'RE THE BEST!

When your child helps out with something at home, be sure to build them up...even if they're still learning to do it! Giving them an area where they feel really successful and offering praise will help them feel like they have purpose and are contributing to the family in a meaningful way. This sense of purpose and contribution will help kids see themselves with loving eyes.

Age Range:	5–8
Skills:	Social contribution, responsibility
Materials:	Situationally dependent
Number of Participants:	1+
Where to Play:	Inside or outside

BEFORE YOU START

★ Identify a task that your child can do independently that contributes to the family. Model the task for them a few times before they take over independently.

HOW TO PLAY

★ Pick one activity or task that your child does to help at home. It could be something like:
  - Matching up socks in the laundry
  - Organizing the shoe rack
  - Drying dishes
  - Organizing the bookshelf
  - Watering the plants

★ Give your child lots of verbal praise for this task! Tell them that they are the best in the family at this specific task. Point out what they do well. For example, you might say, "You found a match for every sock?! Wow! You're the best sock matcher in the whole family!" or "Whoa—did you organize the bookshelf by color? It looks amazing! It's so easy to find books now, and I feel happy when I look at the rainbow shelf. You're the best book organizer in our home!"

(continued on next page)

★ When that task needs to be completed, call on "the best." Remind your child that they are the best person for the job and ask if they'll rise to the challenge.

THINKING BACK AND LOOKING AHEAD
★ How does it feel to be the best at that in our family?
★ How does it feel to do something that really helps our family?

COMMUNITY CONTRIBUTIONS

Get the family together to find ways to meaningfully contribute to the community! This could be doing a beach cleanup, writing kind messages in sidewalk chalk for others to see, or something else that's meaningful to your family and your community. Contributing to the community will help kids develop a sense of purpose and feel good about the important work they're doing.

Age Range:	**5–11**
Skills:	**Social contribution**
Materials:	**Situationally dependent**
Number of Participants:	**1+**
Where to Play:	**Inside or outside**

BEFORE YOU START

★ As a family, brainstorm ways you can meaningfully contribute to the community.

★ Choose an activity that is meaningful to the whole family. If you decide to volunteer at a specific location, be sure to call ahead and make sure that it's okay to bring kids to volunteer.

HOW TO PLAY

★ Choose a community service activity in your community such as:
  • Cleaning up a park or beach
  • Reading to animals at a shelter
  • Organizing donations at a food pantry

★ Bring kids along and encourage them to participate in ways that are appropriate for their ages. As you volunteer, explain to the kids what you are doing and why.

THINKING BACK AND LOOKING AHEAD

★ What did you enjoy about this activity today?

★ What questions do you have about what we did or why?

(continued on next page)

★ How did you feel while we were doing this activity?

★ What other activities would you like to do to serve others?

Here are ten kid-friendly community service activities:

1. Plant trees.

2. Clean up a park.

3. Make cards or art for a senior-care center.

4. Collect items needed by shelters.

5. Write thank-you notes to first responders and healthcare workers.

6. Donate gently used toys and clothes.

7. Make cards for patients at a children's hospital.

8. Adopt a family for the holidays.

9. Help older or disabled neighbors get groceries.

10. Write encouraging words on sidewalks (where permitted).

MAGAZINE COVER STAR

Look into the future….What is your child famous for? Help your child imagine how they will contribute to the world, and create a magazine cover to highlight their contributions and purpose. Thinking about the ways they could change the world will help them see that the sky is the limit for their potential!

Age Range:	**5–11**
Skills:	**Creativity, critical thinking, planning**
Materials:	**Paper, pencil, coloring utensils, glue, scissors, old magazines**
Number of Participants:	**1+**
Where to Play:	**Inside**

BEFORE YOU START

★ Show younger children some magazine covers that show a single person so they can see what it looks like to be featured on one.

HOW TO PLAY

★ Help your child imagine they are on the cover of a magazine because of their contributions to the community or world.
  - What would you be famous for contributing? A new life-saving medicine? Building houses for people in need? Taking in animals who need homes?
★ Have your child draw a picture of themselves on the paper, or print a picture of your child and glue it on the paper.
★ Using old magazines, cut out letters or words to create headlines showing why your child would be on the cover of the magazine. Glue the words around the picture of your child to create a magazine cover.
★ Hang the magazine cover in your home as inspiration to go out and do those amazing things.

(continued on next page)

THINKING BACK AND LOOKING AHEAD

* How does it feel to imagine that you are famous for doing good things for the world?
* How do you feel looking at this magazine cover?
* How will this motivate you to go out and do those things?
* In what other ways might you like to contribute to the world around you?

WHY AND HOW

Kids are famous for asking, "Why?" Give them the "why" and "how" behind the chores they're expected to do to help them understand the purpose and develop a sense of how they are contributing by doing them. This purpose, contribution, and responsibility will help them see themselves with love.

Age Range:	**5–11**
Skills:	**Social contribution, responsibility, cooperation**
Materials:	**None**
Number of Participants:	**The whole family**
Where to Play:	**Inside or outside**

BEFORE YOU START

★ Set expectations for the chores that your child (or children) is expected to do daily or weekly to contribute to the family and to be responsible.

HOW TO PLAY

★ Make a list of your child's chores, or refer to the Household Jobs activity in this chapter.
★ For each chore, explain to your child why they are expected to do it and how it contributes to the family and the home. For example:
  • You are expected to put your toys away at the end of each day when you are finished playing with them. The family needs you to do this so that our floor is clean and so that no one gets hurt. If someone is walking in the living room and your cars are on the floor, they might step on a car and fall! They could get hurt. Putting your toys away helps keep our home clean and helps us all stay safe.
★ Focusing on the reason behind each chore and how their completion of the chore contributes to the family will help them develop a sense of purpose and feel good about the ways they contribute.

THINKING BACK AND LOOKING AHEAD

★ What questions do you still have about how your chores help the family?
★ Are there any other ways you would like to help the family and contribute at home?

HELP WANTED

Have odd jobs around the house? Hire some help! Create a job board for extra jobs at home so that your child can contribute outside of their normal chores. Contributing to the family in meaningful ways will give kids positive feelings, especially when others appreciate their efforts.

Age Range:	**5–11**
Skills:	**Social contribution, responsibility**
Materials:	**Whiteboard, bulletin board, or paper; writing utensils**
Number of Participants:	**The whole family**
Where to Play:	**Inside**

BEFORE YOU START

★ Make a list of jobs or tasks that need to be done around the home that your child can complete independently. These should be jobs that are outside of your child's normal chores.

HOW TO PLAY

★ Make a "Help Wanted" job board on a whiteboard, bulletin board, or paper. If you'd like to offer money or some reward for completing the job, include that on the job listing.
★ Kids can review the job board and choose extra jobs to complete at home.
★ Be sure to offer lots of verbal praise and appreciation! Explain to your child how completing that job helped you or the family.

THINKING BACK AND LOOKING AHEAD

★ Why did you choose that job?
★ How did it feel to help out in that extra way?
★ How does contributing to our family make you feel?
★ In what other ways would you like to contribute to our family?

HOW YOU HELP JENGA

In this activity, kids will play a familiar game with a twist. This game will encourage all family members to think about the ways each person contributes to the group as a whole. Hearing how they help the family will give kids a sense of pride that's foundational to self-love.

Age Range:	**5–11**
Skills:	**Critical thinking, respect, cooperation**
Materials:	**Jenga game, pencil**
Number of Participants:	**The whole family**
Where to Play:	**Inside or outside**

BEFORE YOU START

★ Talk about ways that people help their families. Kids can do things inside the home, like cleaning, telling jokes, or offering hugs, or things outside the home, like teaching a sibling to ride a bike.

HOW TO PLAY

★ Write the names of family members on the Jenga blocks in pencil. There should be a name on every block, so names will be repeated.
★ Play the game by the traditional rules. When a player removes a block from the tower, they will share one way the family member whose name is on the block helps other family members. They might say things like:
  • She helps me pick out my clothes every morning.
  • He helps me take deep breaths when I'm sad.
  • She helps me find my favorite books.
★ Add the block to the top of the tower.
★ Keep playing until the tower falls, and then work together to rebuild it!

THINKING BACK AND LOOKING AHEAD

★ How did it feel to tell someone how they help you?
★ How did it feel to hear how you help other people?
★ In what other ways would you like to help people in our family?

NEIGHBORHOOD BEAUTIFICATION

Taking pride in the neighborhood and feeling connected to others in the area will help kids feel good about themselves and their surroundings. Doing a neighborhood beautification project will boost that feeling of social connectedness, which is a foundation of self-love.

Age Range:	**5–11**
Skills:	**Social contribution, responsibility, problem-solving**
Materials:	**Situationally dependent**
Number of Participants:	**The whole family**
Where to Play:	**In the neighborhood or community**

BEFORE YOU START

★ Talk to your child about what it means to be a good neighbor. For example, you could say, "A good neighbor is someone who cares about the people they live close to and cares about the area where they live. A good neighbor treats others and the area with respect."

HOW TO PLAY

★ As a family or group, make a list of neighborhood beautification projects you could do together to contribute to the community. These could be things like:
  - Planting flowers in a common area (with approval)
  - Picking up trash in the neighborhood
  - Painting a mural on a fence or wall (with approval)
★ Choose one project to do together, and go do it!

THINKING BACK AND LOOKING AHEAD

★ What was fun about this activity?
★ Who in our neighborhood do you think will appreciate it the most?
★ How does it feel to contribute to the neighborhood?
★ In what other ways would you like to give back to our neighborhood?

HOUSEHOLD JOBS

Chores are everyone's responsibility. Help your child contribute in meaningful ways by creating a list of jobs that need doing in your home. Take turns having each family member be in charge of age-appropriate jobs so that everyone develops a sense of purpose and contribution. Contributing to the family in meaningful ways will give kids positive feelings, especially when others appreciate their efforts! Enjoying a sense of purpose can build self-love.

Age Range:	5–11
Skills:	Social contribution, responsibility, cooperation
Materials:	Paper, markers, lamination machine, dry-erase markers (optional)
Number of Participants:	The whole family
Where to Play:	Inside or outside

BEFORE YOU START

* Work together to make a list of jobs at home. Be creative in your job titles to make the tasks sound more fun and important! Here are some examples:
  * Librarian: in charge of putting all books back on the shelf
  * Energy conservationist: in charge of making sure lights are turned off
  * Custodian or facilities manager: in charge of taking out the trash and recycling
  * Zookeeper: in charge of feeding pets
  * Chef: in charge of making after-school snacks

HOW TO PLAY

* On paper, write all the household jobs you identified. Laminate this paper if possible.
* With a dry-erase marker (or regular marker if paper is not laminated), write the name of a family member beside each job.
* For one week, that family member is in charge of that job. At the end of the week, switch jobs.

(continued on next page)

THINKING BACK AND LOOKING AHEAD

★ Which job is your favorite? Your least favorite?
★ How does it feel to know others are counting on you to do your job?
★ What might happen if you didn't do your job?

PACK YOUR LUNCH

What's for lunch? Let your child decide! Being in charge of packing their own lunch is a big responsibility, but it will let them make a tangible contribution as they take ownership of the process. Finding success with an important job like this will boost self-esteem. Bonus: If they pack it themselves, they'll be more likely to eat it, because the choice was theirs.

Age Range:	**6–11**
Skills:	**Social contribution, responsibility**
Materials:	**Paper, writing utensil, lunch food, lunch box**
Number of Participants:	**1+**
Where to Play:	**Inside**

BEFORE YOU START

★ Talk with your child about what should be included in the lunch. You can write out a checklist or menu of options for them to use as a guide.
  • For example, for a checklist, write that the lunch box must include:
    • 1 protein
    • 1 fruit
    • 1 veggie
    • 1 grain
    • 1 snack
    • 1 drink
  • Or make a menu of options for each item. For example, kids might be able to choose their protein from these options:
    • Turkey and cheese roll-up
    • Pulled rotisserie chicken
    • Peanut butter and jelly sandwich
★ Prep items over the weekend so it's easy for kids to make choices. Organize the refrigerator so they can easily see the fruit options or easily pick up a bag of carrots or a container of cherry tomatoes.

(continued on next page)

HOW TO PLAY

★ On school nights, give your child free rein to pack their own lunch... within boundaries.
★ Give them a menu of choices or guidelines to follow as they pack.
★ Give the lunch a quick check before packing it away to make sure they have everything they need.

THINKING BACK AND LOOKING AHEAD

★ How does it feel to be in charge of packing your own lunch?
★ What other tasks would you like to be in charge of?

PACK YOUR SUITCASE

Heading out on a trip? Let your child try to pack their own suitcase! Taking ownership of the task and having a clear mission can help kids feel a sense of purpose. Seeing these positive qualities of purpose and trustworthiness in themselves will build up their self-love.

Age Range:	**7–11**
Skills:	**Social contribution, responsibility**
Materials:	**Paper, pencil, suitcase**
Number of Participants:	**1+**
Where to Play:	**Inside**

BEFORE YOU START
* Demonstrate for your child how to use a checklist:
  * Read one item on the list.
  * Pack the item in your suitcase.
  * Check off the item so that you remember you already packed it.
* Demonstrate for your child how to pack a suitcase. Show them how to fold clothes, put liquids in a bag, or tuck socks inside of tennis shoes!

HOW TO PLAY
* Together with your child, write a packing list for the trip. You can do this by item (e.g., five shirts, five pairs of shorts) or by day (e.g., Monday: outfit for being outside, bathing suit, tennis shoes).
* Let your child use the packing list to pack their own suitcase.
* Before the trip, do a final review with your child to make sure they got all the items on the list.
* Give your child lots of verbal praise for their efforts and let them know how much their independence on this task helps.

THINKING BACK AND LOOKING AHEAD
* What strategies did you use to help yourself stay on track for packing?
* How did it feel to accomplish this task?

BECAUSE I CAN...

What skills and qualities does your kid have? How can they use them for good? This activity will help kids connect their qualities and skills to meaningful ways they can give to others. Being able to contribute or give to others will help kids feel good about themselves.

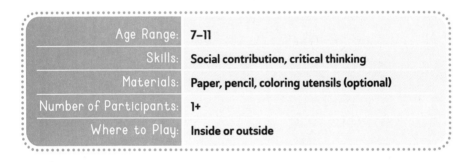

Age Range:	**7–11**
Skills:	**Social contribution, critical thinking**
Materials:	**Paper, pencil, coloring utensils (optional)**
Number of Participants:	**1+**
Where to Play:	**Inside or outside**

BEFORE YOU START

★ Talk about what it means to contribute or give. You could say something like, "Contributing means that we do our part. Giving means that we give our time or give things to people who need them. When we contribute and give, we help others, and we can also feel good about ourselves for doing good."

HOW TO PLAY

★ Turn the paper horizontally. Draw a vertical line in the middle of the paper. Label the left side "Because I Can/Am." Label the right side "I Can Give."

★ On the left side, help your child brainstorm qualities they have or skills they have.

★ On the right side, help your child think of ways they can use those qualities or skills to give to others. For example:

Because I Can/Am	I Can Give
Because I can read,	I can give to my sister by reading to her.
Because I am helpful and like being outside,	I can give my time to our older neighbors to help them with yard work.

* You may want to let your child draw a picture or symbol next to each thing they wrote as a visual reminder.
* Use this list to help your child take action to contribute to others!

THINKING BACK AND LOOKING AHEAD

* How does it feel to think about the ways you can use your skills and qualities to give back to others?
* What action would you like to take first?
* How will it feel to give to others?

PASSION PROJECT

In this activity, you'll give your child space to share their passion and where it's taking them. They can create a personalized project that hones in on their interests. Feeling a sense of purpose and passion will help offer kids some direction and motivation, which translates into feelings of self-love.

Age Range:	8–11
Skills:	Self-reflection, communication
Materials:	Situationally dependent
Number of Participants:	The whole family or group
Where to Play:	Inside or outside

BEFORE YOU START

★ Talk about what a passion is. You could say something like, "Passions are things that we care deeply about and things that mean a lot to us."
★ Talk about what "purpose" means. For example, "A sense of purpose is when we feel driven or motivated toward something."
★ Discuss how they are related, saying something like, "Our passions are linked to our purpose. The things we care the most about drive our purpose. We are motivated to do things to support our passions."
★ Share your own passions with your child. Tell them how these are linked to your own sense of purpose. For example:
  • I am passionate about animals! I want to keep them healthy and happy. That's why I became a vet technician. I feel a sense of purpose when I am at work helping animals feel better.
  • I am passionate about protecting our environment and planet. I feel a sense of purpose when I take our recyclables to be sorted, because I know they won't be in a landfill and harming our planet.

HOW TO PLAY

★ Help your child identify their passion. Ask them questions like:
  • What things do you care the most about?
  • When do you feel most energized?

- When do you feel like you are doing something important and meaningful?
- What is something you wish you could learn or talk about all the time?

★ Let your child create a "passion project" to share, explain, and convey their passion. They can share what their passion is, how they became interested in it, who encouraged them to follow it, and what they want to do next to explore their passion. A passion project can be a:
  - Poster
  - Song
  - Skit
  - Speech
  - Poem

★ When the project is ready, share it with the whole family or group.

THINKING BACK AND LOOKING AHEAD

★ How does it feel to share your passion with everyone?

★ How can we support you as you explore your passion?

★ What else do you want to know or learn about your passion?

★ What actions or steps would you like to take to support your passion?

INSPIRATIONAL PEOPLE PROJECT

Encourage kids to learn about inspirational people. Learning more about the passions, purpose, and contributions of other exceptional people in the world will encourage your child to look inward and discover their own passions, purpose, and contributions. As kids learn more about the inspirational stories of others, encourage them to be loving toward themselves in their own stories when they make mistakes or face obstacles.

Age Range:	**9–11**
Skills:	**Critical thinking, curiosity**
Materials:	**Computer, videos, books**
Number of Participants:	**1+**
Where to Play:	**At home or the library**

BEFORE YOU START

★ Talk about what "inspirational" means. You could say something like, "'Inspirational' means someone or something makes other people want to do the same or similar things. When people inspire us, they make us want to try new things, do good things, keep working hard, or learn more things!"

HOW TO PLAY

★ Choose an inspirational person to research. Spend time with your child reading about the person or watching videos or documentaries about the person. Here are a few ideas for inspirational young people to learn more about:
  • Kelvin Doe, an inventor
  • Greta Thunberg, an environmental activist
  • Jahkil Jackson, who helps provide relief for the homeless
  • Malala Yousafzai, a girls' and women's education advocate
  • Kalpana Chawla, an astronaut (Note: She died in the *Columbia* explosion.)

★ Talk about how the person is or was inspiring by asking questions such as:
  • What did they do or say that was inspiring?
  • What did they inspire others to do?

THINKING BACK AND LOOKING AHEAD
★ Are you feeling inspired? What are you feeling inspired to do?
★ How might you like to inspire others?
★ What qualities do you have that could inspire others?

CHAPTER 7

INFLUENCE

WHAT IS INFLUENCE?

Influence is a child's capacity to produce outcomes, actions, and behaviors in others. Kids develop a sense of influence as they see their behaviors, cries, or silliness impact the behaviors and reactions of the adults around them. As kids grow and have more outside-the-home experiences, they'll have more opportunities for influence, and you can help them learn how to use it for good.

HOW DOES INFLUENCE RELATE TO SELF-LOVE?

When kids see that they have the ability to influence the people and world around them, they feel powerful and important! People who have a big influence over others tend to feel better about themselves than people who feel like they have no control over events around them, especially when they use that power and influence in a positive way.

When kids feel good about the positive impact they have on others, they feel good about themselves too. When kids positively influence and contribute to their circles, they can start to feel good about who they are on the inside and how they show that on the outside.

WHAT DOES INFLUENCE LOOK AND SOUND LIKE?

The outward demonstration of positive influence involves taking positive actions to make changes in the surrounding environment. Some examples of outward demonstrations of influence include:

* Making suggestions for changes to routines or practices
* Encouraging others with gestures or words
* Speaking up for what is right
* Advocating for oneself and others

INFLUENCE IN KID-FRIENDLY TERMS

To explain influence to your kid, try saying something like this:

You get to make a lot of choices in your life. You get to choose your words and choose your actions. The really cool thing is that your words and actions can impact other people. Your words and actions can encourage other people to choose good and positive words and actions too. That's called having an influence. "Influence" means that you can use your words and actions to make changes in the world around you. You can influence people by encouraging them or helping them. You can influence our family by making suggestions for how we do things or by contributing to the activities that we do.

LOOKING AHEAD

In this chapter, you'll find activities that encourage kids to speak up and do good. You'll also find activities that inspire kids to leave positive marks on their circles of influence, no matter how big or small.

THIS OR THAT

Everyone wants to feel like they have a choice, and kids are no exception. Give your child developmentally appropriate choices to give them a sense of influence. Feeling like they are impacting their environment, even in small ways, will boost their sense of self.

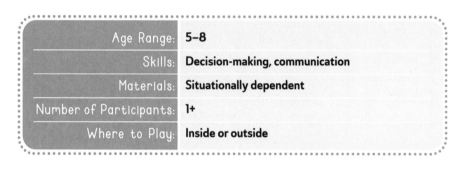

Age Range:	**5–8**
Skills:	**Decision-making, communication**
Materials:	**Situationally dependent**
Number of Participants:	**1+**
Where to Play:	**Inside or outside**

BEFORE YOU START

★ Think about areas of life in which you are comfortable giving your child the freedom to choose. These choices should be positive alternatives, which means that both options given to the child should be things that caregivers are okay with. So instead of saying, "Do you want to keep lying on the floor screaming, or do you want to get up and talk about it?" say, "Would you like to talk about how you feel, or would you like to hug your stuffed dino?" This gives the child the freedom to choose while also conveying that the undesired behavior (screaming on the floor) is not an option.

HOW TO PLAY

★ In everyday tasks, offer your child choices. Make sure both choices are positive or desirable choices that you would want them to choose. Here are some examples of ways to incorporate choices into everyday life:
  • Would you like to have oatmeal or cereal for breakfast?
  • Should we hop or skip to the bathroom to brush teeth?
  • Should we sing along to songs in the car or just listen?
★ For younger children, offer two choices. Older children may be able to manage three or four options.

THINKING BACK AND LOOKING AHEAD

★ How does it feel to make choices?
★ What other kinds of choices would you like to be able to make?

SUGGESTION BOX

Does your kid have any great ideas? Put them in the suggestion box! Having an avenue for proposing new ideas for the family, class, or group will give your child a sense of influence, which will in turn give them a self-esteem boost. When they feel good about the ways in which they can influence a group, they feel good about themselves too.

Age Range:	**5–11**
Skills:	**Decision-making, responsibility, communication**
Materials:	**Shoebox or other small box, craft supplies (stickers, glitter, markers, etc.), paper, pencils**
Number of Participants:	**The whole family or group**
Where to Play:	**Inside**

BEFORE YOU START

★ Talk about what a suggestion is with younger kids. You can say something like, "A suggestion is an idea for how to do something or an idea for a way to change something. People may want to make a suggestion when something makes them feel uncomfortable, sad, or left out. They may also want to make a suggestion when something they value is not prioritized."

★ Talk about how to write a suggestion. It could look something like this:
  • We usually do _____. I think it would be better to do _____ because _____.
  • When we do _____, could we also do _____?
  • I suggest that we _____ as a family/class/group.
  • When we do _____, I feel _____. Instead, could we do _____?

★ You may want to premake some cards with these fill-in-the-blank prompts for younger kids.

★ Give kids some examples of suggestions:
  • I suggest that we have a family movie night every week.
  • I suggest that we have a snack before homework instead of after homework because it's easier for me to concentrate when I am not hungry.

(continued on next page)

* Remind kids that all suggestions might not lead to changes. Let them know that all suggestions will at least be discussed and considered as a family or group.

HOW TO PLAY

* Create a suggestion box with a shoebox, plastic bin, or something similar. Decorate it as a family or group.
* When a member of the family or group has a suggestion for a way to improve a family process or a suggestion for a change the group could make as a whole, they can write it on paper and put it in the suggestion box.
* Designate a day of the week or month to review the suggestions in the box, talk about them as a family or group, and take a vote on the suggestion.

THINKING BACK AND LOOKING AHEAD

* How did it feel to share your suggestion with the family or group?
* What feelings led to your suggestion?
* How does it feel to talk about your suggestion as a whole family or group?

PLAN THE MENU

Menu planning doesn't always have to be an adult's task—let your child help! Invite them to plan the menu for one meal, one weekend, or the whole week. Having an influence over the family will give them an opportunity to feel impactful and confident in their contributions. Having an important role will translate to feelings of worth and love!

Age Range:	5–11
Skills:	Planning, decision-making, responsibility
Materials:	Paper, pencils
Number of Participants:	1+
Where to Play:	Inside

BEFORE YOU START

* Talk about why you plan a menu as a family. For example, planning balanced meals will help nourish everyone, and we can save money and time by shopping for everything at once.
* For younger children, create a menu of options. You may want to include pictures of the meals as well.
* For older children, create guidelines for what to include in each meal (such as a protein or meat, grain, veggies, etc.).

HOW TO PLAY

* With a little guidance, let your child write down the nightly, weekend, or weekday menu. Be sure to set limits that work for your schedule (e.g., "We can make pancakes on Sunday but not on a busy weekday morning.")
* Give your child parameters of what to include for each meal, such as one protein, one grain, and two veggies. But let them choose the dish that falls into each category.
* For younger children, you may want to provide a menu of options and let them choose from the menu, then help them write it down. For example, give them a list of ten meals your family likes, and let them choose three for the weekend dinner menu.
* Stick to the menu they picked.

(continued on next page)

THINKING BACK AND LOOKING AHEAD

* ★ What was it like to plan the menu for our family?
* ★ How did it feel to be able to influence the plan?
* ★ What other things would you like to plan?

GENEROSITY DAY

In this activity, you'll designate one day a month as Generosity Day. Giving to others will give kids a sense of influence and pride in themselves and their ability to spread kindness in the world.

Age Range:	**5–11**
Skills:	**Planning, social contribution, responsibility**
Materials:	**Situationally dependent**
Number of Participants:	**The whole family**
Where to Play:	**Inside or outside**

BEFORE YOU START
★ Talk about what it means to be generous. You could say, "'Generous' means that we freely and enthusiastically give to others or share with others."

HOW TO PLAY
★ Choose one day a month for Generosity Day. On that day, do as many generous activities as possible. These activities can be at home, around the neighborhood, or in the community. Here are some examples of activities you could do:
- Share toys with siblings.
- Choose gently used toys or clothes to donate.
- Create art and share it with neighbors.
- Bake cookies for neighbors.
- Give time by helping older family members or neighbors with chores.

THINKING BACK AND LOOKING AHEAD
★ How did it feel to give to others?
★ What was your favorite way to be generous?
★ How do you feel about yourself after being generous to others?
★ In what other ways would you like to be generous?

MAKE A CASE

Whether it's a later bedtime, a pet, or a trip to the toy store, kids are always asking for something. When kids want to do something, buy something, or go somewhere, have them "make a case" for what they want. Presenting the details, feelings, and facts of their side of things will not only help kids build great conversational and presentation skills, but also give them a confidence boost when they feel like they are influencing their own outcomes.

Age Range:	7–11
Skills:	Communication, critical thinking, public speaking
Materials:	None
Number of Participants:	The whole family
Where to Play:	Inside or outside

BEFORE YOU START

* Talk about what it means to "make a case" for something. You could say, "'Making a case' means that you explain your reasoning for why you should get to do something, get to have something, or get to make a change."
* Help your child plan their case using prompts like this:
  • What I would like to get/do/change:
  • Why this is important to me:
  • Supporting fact or detail #1:
  • Supporting fact or detail #2:
  • How I'll be responsible for it:
* Here's an example:

What I would like to get/do/change:	I would like to bike to school instead of being dropped off in the car.
Why this is important to me:	My friends bike to school together, and I want to spend more time with them.

Supporting fact or detail #1:	Biking together with friends will be safer than biking alone.
Supporting fact or detail #2:	Biking is exercise, so I'll be healthier.
How I'll be responsible for it:	I'll wear all my protective gear and follow the rules of the road.

HOW TO PLAY

* When kids want to buy something new, make a change, or do something new, tell them to make a case for it.
* Give kids time to prepare what they want to say and how they want to say it.
* Designate a time for them to present their ideas to the family, and hear them out!
* Consider their ideas and give them feedback and a response.

THINKING BACK AND LOOKING AHEAD

* How did it feel to prepare to make your case?
* How did it feel to make your case to the family?
* Why do you think it's important to share this information with us?
* How does it feel when your idea is supported by the family?

INSPIRATIONAL QUOTE

As kids learn how they can influence others, they might be inspired by the words of other leaders. Find motivational quotes to share as a family or group (or create your own!), and share how the quotes impact you. Focusing on positive messages and sharing those with others will give your child a chance to feel like they are positively impacting others.

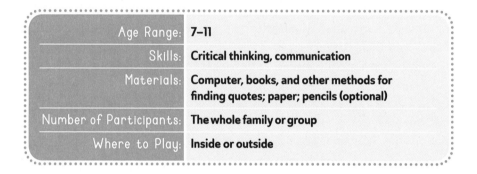

Age Range:	**7–11**
Skills:	**Critical thinking, communication**
Materials:	**Computer, books, and other methods for finding quotes; paper; pencils (optional)**
Number of Participants:	**The whole family or group**
Where to Play:	**Inside or outside**

BEFORE YOU START

★ Talk about what a motivational quote is. You might say something like, "A motivational quote is something that someone said with the intention of encouraging others or motivating them to do something. Some motivational quotes encourage us to work toward our goals, some encourage us to persevere through hard things, and some encourage us to do good things."

HOW TO PLAY

★ Designate a day of the week or month to share your motivational quotes as a family or group.
★ Each participant will find and bring a motivational quote to share.
★ Each person will read the quote to the group and share how the quote impacts them or how they are encouraged by it.
★ If you would like, create a motivational quote wall. Everyone can write or print out the quotes they found and hang them up!

THINKING BACK AND LOOKING AHEAD

★ What was it like to share your quote with the family or group?
★ What do you hope others will get/feel/do as a result of hearing your quote?
★ How does it feel to motivate or encourage other people?

MOTIVATIONAL SPEAKING

Teach kids to use their words for good. When a big event is coming up, give your child the chance to perform a motivational speech to encourage others and influence them positively. They'll feel good about their impact!

Age Range:	**7–11**
Skills:	**Communication, planning**
Materials:	**Paper, writing utensil (optional)**
Number of Participants:	**2+**
Where to Play:	**Inside or outside**

BEFORE YOU START

★ Talk about what it means to be motivational. You could say something like, "Being motivational means that we encourage people and inspire them to keep going or do something hard. Giving a motivational speech means that we plan motivational things to say to people to encourage them."

★ Watch examples of motivational speeches online. Find videos from Kid President or other motivational youth on TED Talks.

HOW TO PLAY

★ Let your child give a motivational speech to help others through a difficult or special time. Here are some examples:
  - A big sports game
  - A Saturday filled with chores and errands
  - A medical appointment
  - An important test at school

★ Help your child make a plan for what they want to say, and guide them through writing a speech if they would like to have a written copy. Include things like:
  - An encouraging quote
  - Three things to remember when you're facing the upcoming challenge
  - An anecdote about a time when they went through something similar

(continued on next page)

- Final encouraging words
* Set aside a time for your child to give their motivational speech, and listen attentively.

THINKING BACK AND LOOKING AHEAD

* How did it feel to give a motivational speech?
* How do you think the people who listened felt?
* Who else would you like to give a motivational speech to?

SCHEDULE THE WEEKEND

What are we doing this weekend? You decide! Let your child plan **some of** the family's weekend activities for a sense of influence and accomplishment. Kids will build self-love through the confidence they gain taking on **import-** ant roles like this.

Age Range:	**7–11**
Skills:	**Planning, decision-making, responsibility**
Materials:	**Paper, pencils**
Number of Participants:	**1+**
Where to Play:	**Inside**

BEFORE YOU START
* Talk about the balance of activities for the weekend. It's great to relax, spend some quality time together, and have fun, but still take care of responsibilities.
* Make a list of "must-do" activities for the weekend and "can-do" activities for kids to choose from.

HOW TO PLAY
* With a little guidance, let your child plan the weekend activities. Give your child guidelines for things that must be done and fun things they can choose from. You could include things like:
  * Saturday: all regular chores, one family board game, one outdoor activity, one movie
  * Sunday: one visit to a family member, one outdoor activity, one restaurant, one art activity
* Let your child fill in the blanks with their activity choices, and stick to their plan.

THINKING BACK AND LOOKING AHEAD
* What was it like to plan the weekend for our family?
* How did it feel to be able to influence the plan?
* What other things would you like to plan?

HOW MANY HATS?

Everyone wears different hats every day, even kids! In this activity, you'll challenge kids to imagine how they can positively impact others in each of their roles. Expanding kids' view of themselves and their potential influence gives them more avenues to self-love.

Age Range:	7–11
Skills:	Critical thinking, planning, social contribution
Materials:	Paper, pencil
Number of Participants:	1+
Where to Play:	Inside

BEFORE YOU START

★ Talk about what a role is. You could say something like, "A role is a position or a title we have. One person can have a lot of roles. We have roles at home within our families, roles at school, roles in the community, and roles anywhere else we go."

★ Talk about what it means to positively impact others. Say, "Positively impacting others means that we do and say good things that make people feel good, encourage others, or build them up!"

HOW TO PLAY

★ On paper, draw a hat for each role your child has (e.g., child, sibling, grandchild, cousin, student, soccer teammate).

★ Under each hat, challenge your child to list at least two ways that they can positively impact others in this role. Here's an example:

Hat I Wear	How I Can Positively Impact Others in This Role
Son	Say nice and encouraging things to my mom Draw art to make Mom smile
Student	Help my classmates when they are confused Include people who get left out sometimes
Teammate	Cheer on my teammates Be a good sport

* Set a goal to actually do the things they identified as ways to positively impact others, and check in regularly on how it's going.

THINKING BACK AND LOOKING AHEAD

* What is it like to think about all the roles you have?
* Were you surprised by all the ways that you can positively impact other people?
* How does it feel to actually do those things?
* In what other ways would you like to positively impact others?

WHAT'S YOUR TAKE?

Have you asked your kid what they think about what's going on in the world? Give your kid a chance to share their opinions and thoughts about current events. Knowing that adults value their opinions will give kids a sense of influence and an appreciation for the value of their own thoughts and voice.

Age Range:	**9–11**
Skills:	**Critical thinking, communication**
Materials:	**None**
Number of Participants:	**1+**
Where to Play:	**Inside or outside**

BEFORE YOU START
★ Choose kid-friendly news outlets and news stories to get information on current events.

HOW TO PLAY
★ When you're listening to a news report on the radio in the car, watching the news at home, or just having a conversation about current events, ask your kid for their take. Give them a moment to share their opinion on what's going on.
★ Ask questions like:
  • What do you think about what's going on?
  • What would you do if you were in charge of this?
  • How do you think people could fix this situation?
  • What feelings do you think the people involved have?
★ Highlight and praise interesting thoughts or points that they make.

THINKING BACK AND LOOKING AHEAD
★ Do you like talking about these kinds of things with me?
★ What other things would you like for me to ask your opinion on?

IDENTITY

WHAT IS IDENTITY?

Identity is the basis for a child's sense of self. It encapsulates their beliefs, culture, roles, values, experiences, interests, relationships, memories, and more. In exploring identity, people often pose questions like "Who are you?" and "Who do you want to be?" As kids grow, have new experiences, learn more about their culture, and formulate their own values, beliefs, and interests, they'll have more opportunities to explore their identities.

HOW DOES IDENTITY RELATE TO SELF-LOVE?

For kids, understanding who they are and feeling comfortable with their values, beliefs, and interests is where identity and self-love intersect. As kids discover more about who they are and think ahead to who they want to become, they'll receive messages from the people and community around them about whether their identity is accepted. When kids feel confident in their own identities and also supported by those around them in those identities, they receive the message that they are valuable and worthy of love. Kids internalize this message and translate it to self-love when they can celebrate their own personal identities with the safety of acceptance from those around them.

WHAT DOES IDENTITY LOOK AND SOUND LIKE?

The outward demonstration of identity involves expressing your interests, values, beliefs, and more. Some examples of outward demonstrations of identity include:

* Engaging in important cultural traditions or practices
* Wearing a shirt of a favorite band, team, or concept
* Standing up for things that are important to you
* Creating artwork that is representative of yourself

IDENTITY IN KID-FRIENDLY TERMS

To explain identity to your kid, try saying something like this:

As you get older, you'll learn a lot about the world and yourself. You'll try new things. You'll figure out what really matters most to you. You'll have experiences that shape who you are as a person, because they will give you strong feelings. You'll begin to understand who you are as a person and who you want to be.

Identity is what makes you who you are. Your identity is the connection of the things you like to do, the things you believe about yourself and the world, your background, your values and how you want to treat others and the world, and the things you are passionate about. Your identity is what makes you you!

LOOKING AHEAD

In this chapter, you'll find activities that encourage kids to explore different aspects of their identities. These activities can inspire kids to celebrate their unique qualities and all the special things that make them the amazing people they are.

LUCKY TO BE ME

Everyone can experience a little luck of the Irish with this activity. You'll craft a shamrock or four-leaf clover with reasons that your child feels lucky to be themselves. Reflecting on reasons they feel lucky to be themselves will remind them of all the amazing qualities and skills they have and give them a self-love boost.

Age Range:	**5–7**
Skills:	**Self-reflection, gratitude, mindfulness**
Materials:	**Paper, coloring utensils, writing utensil, picture frame (optional)**
Number of Participants:	**1+**
Where to Play:	**Inside**

BEFORE YOU START

★ With your child, look up the history of the four-leaf clover and how it's connected to luck.

★ Talk about what "lucky" means. You could say, "Feeling lucky means we feel fortunate to have things, have experiences, do things, have skills, and so on."

HOW TO PLAY

★ On paper, draw a four-leaf clover (or print it out from a template if you prefer).

★ On each leaf, help your child write a reason they feel lucky to be them! They might include things like:

- I have a great family.
- I live in a beautiful place.
- I have a cute puppy.
- I have a safe, warm home.

★ Let your child color or decorate the shamrock.

★ Hang it somewhere highly visible, or frame it for your child!

(continued on next page)

THINKING BACK AND LOOKING AHEAD

★ Was it easy or difficult to think of the reasons you feel lucky to be you?

★ How do you think your life would be different if you spent more time thinking about the things you do have in your life instead of things you don't have?

★ How do you feel when you look at your shamrock?

I AM...

You shine like the sun! This art project will highlight all the things your child is. Spending time thinking about positive adjectives to describe themselves will help kids focus on their best qualities, honor the characteristics they embody, and love themselves.

Age Range:	**5–8**
Skills:	**Self-reflection**
Materials:	**Plain paper, coloring utensils, and writing utensil; or construction paper, scissors, glue, and writing utensil; or a computer with an online sketching program**
Number of Participants:	**1+**
Where to Play:	**Inside or virtually**

BEFORE YOU START

★ Talk with your child about how they would complete the sentence "I am..." Discuss positive adjectives that could describe them. You may want to have a list on hand of positive adjectives, character traits, or qualities that you can review together. Talk about what each quality means, and ask your child to share examples of how they embody that quality.

HOW TO PLAY

★ Draw a circle for a sun, or cut out a circle from construction paper. In the circle, write, "I am..."

★ Draw rays coming out from the circle, or cut out rectangles to represent sun rays. On the rays, have your child write positive qualities that describe them. For example, your child's sun might say, "I am..."
  • Brave
  • Kind
  • Creative
  • Loving
  • A good big sister

(continued on next page)

* To do this virtually, use an online sketching program, such as the sketching feature included in Zoom.
* You may even want to make it a daily or weekly routine to have your child say these things aloud, as a type of positive affirmation.

THINKING BACK AND LOOKING AHEAD

* How does it feel to think about your positive qualities?
* How will you feel when you look at this art hanging up?
* Can you think of a time when it might be helpful to look at this and say these things out loud?

If you want an alternative idea, you could also make a rainbow. Simply write, "I am_" on a cloud, and on each color of the rainbow, write a word to complete the sentence. Or write, "I am_" in the center of a star and use the points of the star to write the qualities.

NAME ACROSTIC

What's in a name? Lots of positive qualities! Create an acrostic poem with your child, highlighting positive traits or qualities they have for each letter of their name. Embedding positive qualities within their name will help them solidify their identity visually and mentally.

Age Range:	**5–8**
Skills:	**Self-reflection, creativity**
Materials:	**Paper, pencil**
Number of Participants:	**1+**
Where to Play:	**Inside**

BEFORE YOU START

Talk with your child about character traits, or qualities that describe a person, their actions, the way they treat others, and so on. Use examples that are relatable by describing a character from your child's favorite book or movie.

HOW TO PLAY

* Have your child write their name vertically on the left side of a piece of paper.
* For each letter of their name, have your child write a positive quality or character trait that describes them. Here's an example for a child named Danny:
  - Determined
  - Artistic
  - Nice
  - Nature lover
  - Yogi
* Display the finished product somewhere your child will see it often.

THINKING BACK AND LOOKING AHEAD

* How does it feel to think about your positive qualities?
* How will you feel when you look at your poem hanging up?
* Can you think of a time when it might be helpful to look at this and say these things out loud?

NAME ORIGIN STORY

Every child's name is special. Knowing the meaning behind their name can give kids a stronger sense of identity, which can help solidify their view of themselves and contribute to feelings of self-love.

Age Range:	**5–11**
Skills:	**Self-reflection**
Materials:	**None are necessary, but a search engine can be helpful if you would like to look up historical origins of your child's name**
Number of Participants:	**1+**
Where to Play:	**Inside or virtually**

BEFORE YOU START
★ Reflect on how your child's name was chosen, what it means, and what you'd like for them to know about it.
★ If your child joined your family through fostering or adoption, spend some time researching their name, the cultural origins behind it, and so on.

HOW TO PLAY
★ Have a conversation with your child about their name. Tell them how it was chosen; what it means to you; any historical, cultural, or familial significance; and so on. If you have special family heirlooms or pictures that relate to their name origin story, share those too.
★ Let your child ask questions.

THINKING BACK AND LOOKING AHEAD
★ How does it feel to hear your name origin story?
★ How do you feel about yourself knowing the meaning of your name?
★ How does it change the way you think or feel about your name?

FAMILY TREE

A family tree is a really powerful visual representation of the members of your family. Seeing their spot on the family tree can help them feel a sense of belonging and connection, which provides a solid foundation for self-love.

Age Range:	**5–11**
Skills:	**Self-reflection**
Materials:	**Paper; pencil; coloring utensils; printer, scissors, and glue (optional); leaf stickers (optional); or use a family tree software tool instead of all the physical materials**
Number of Participants:	**The whole family**
Where to Play:	**Inside or virtually**

BEFORE YOU START
★ Spend some time researching your family tree if you aren't familiar with generations. Gather pictures and think about stories you might want to tell about family members or special memories they have with your child.

HOW TO PLAY
★ Draw a tree. Use the branches to represent parents, grandparents, aunts, uncles, cousins, and so on. Or look online for a family tree template you can print out and fill in. (If you prefer, you can do this activity on a computer using genealogy software.)
★ If you can print pictures of the people in your family, add them to the tree. As you add people to the tree, share memories or let your child share about special times they spent with that person.
★ Let your child help decorate the tree by drawing leaves.
★ Hang your family tree somewhere highly visible for your family to enjoy.

THINKING BACK AND LOOKING AHEAD
★ What is it like to see our family tree? How do you feel when you look at it?
★ What is it like to see where you fit in on the family tree?

PIECES OF ME

Identity has so many different components. Show your child this concept visually by making a puzzle that represents all the important pieces of their identity. This activity showcases the depth of your child's personality and selfhood so they can appreciate and love all parts of themselves.

Age Range:	**5–11**
Skills:	**Self-reflection, creativity**
Materials:	**Paper, writing utensil or printer, scissors, coloring utensils, tape, small poster board**
Number of Participants:	**1+**
Where to Play:	**Inside**

BEFORE YOU START
* Help your child make a list of the beliefs, ideals, people, activities, and things that are most important to them. Brainstorm how they can represent these things with words, symbols, or pictures.

HOW TO PLAY
* Draw or print a jigsaw puzzle template on paper.
* Cut the pieces apart.
* Your child will decorate each piece to represent an area of their life that is important to them. They could have pieces that represent:
  * Religious beliefs
  * An important group or team
  * Their family and friends
  * Their favorite hobbies
* Help your child reassemble the puzzle using tape on a small poster board. Title it "Pieces of Me."

THINKING BACK AND LOOKING AHEAD
* What's it like to see all these things that matter most to you in your puzzle?
* How do all these things work together to shape who you are?
* How do you think you would feel if one of these pieces were missing?
* How can I help you keep these pieces strong?

THE PERSON WHO...

What impact do you want to have? Help your child spend time reflecting on how they want to impact others by identifying how they want others to describe them in the future. Reflecting on how they can impact others will help your child envision their identity in action and help them feel more positively about where they're heading.

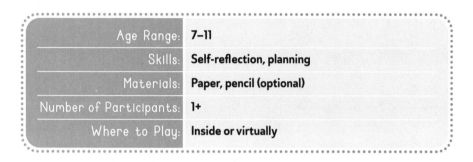

Age Range:	**7–11**
Skills:	**Self-reflection, planning**
Materials:	**Paper, pencil (optional)**
Number of Participants:	**1+**
Where to Play:	**Inside or virtually**

BEFORE YOU START
★ Talk about how you remember other people. Describe for your child a person who is memorable and meaningful to you. For example, you might say, "My grandmother was the person who always listened when I was sad" or "My best friend, Charlie, was the person who knew exactly what encouraging words I needed to hear."

HOW TO PLAY
★ Help your child complete the following sentence about themselves from other people's perspectives. You can set it up with the sentence "He/she/they is/are the person who..."
★ Encourage them to think about how they want others to describe them, what positive traits they hope others will use, or what actions they hope others will notice from their behavior.
★ If you want, have your child write the sentence on paper, and hang it somewhere highly visible so they can see it and reflect on it often.

THINKING BACK AND LOOKING AHEAD
★ What is it like to think about how others might describe you?
★ Why did you choose these words/actions?
★ How can you help others see you this way?
★ How can this sentence be helpful for you in the future?

PERSONAL MOTTO

Mottos aren't just for companies or commercials. Having a grounding statement that highlights their values and what they believe to be true will help kids feel solid in their identities and develop self-love.

Age Range:	**7–11**
Skills:	**Self-reflection**
Materials:	**Paper, pencil**
Number of Participants:	**1+**
Where to Play:	**Inside**

BEFORE YOU START

★ Talk about what a motto is. You could say something like, "A motto is a sentence or statement that summarizes the beliefs or guiding principles of a person or group."

★ Spend some time helping your child reflect on these things with the following questions:
  • How do you believe you should treat others?
  • How do you believe you should treat yourself?
  • What do you want to show the world with your actions and words?

HOW TO PLAY

★ Help your child create a personal motto. Here are a few examples:
  • Be kind, be respectful, be curious.
  • Treat others the way you want to be treated, and learn as much as you can.
  • Look for the good, and if you can't find it, be the good.

★ Have your child write the motto on paper and display it somewhere highly visible.

★ Encourage your child to read it or say it aloud every day.

THINKING BACK AND LOOKING AHEAD

★ What is your favorite thing about your motto?

★ How does it feel to say it out loud?

★ Can you think of times when it would be helpful to say your motto?

★ How will your motto help you?

STORY OF ME

In this activity, you'll help your child write their own story about who they are, how they got here, and where they're going. Thinking about who they are now and who they want to be will help kids formulate a full picture of their identity and celebrate their growth with love.

Age Range:	**7–11**
Skills:	**Self-reflection, creativity, communication**
Materials:	**Notebook or paper, writing utensil, coloring utensils (optional); or use voice-to-text software instead of physical materials**
Number of Participants:	**The whole family**
Where to Play:	**Inside**

BEFORE YOU START

* Read age-appropriate autobiographies with your child to give them an idea of how life stories are told in the first person.
* Help your child brainstorm important things to include in their own life story with questions like:
  * What qualities, skills, or values do you have?
  * Why do you have those qualities, skills, or values? Did someone encourage you to develop those? Did you have experiences that helped you develop those?
  * What are some important experiences that have shaped who you are?
  * Where do you see yourself in the future? What kind of person are you?

HOW TO PLAY

* In a notebook or on blank paper, your child will write their life story (so far!). For younger children, you may choose to have them dictate the story while you write it for them, or use voice-to-text software on a tablet or computer.
* They can include important memories, supportive people, and impactful experiences.
* If your child wants to illustrate the story, they can do that too!
* Read their story together as a family.

THINKING BACK AND LOOKING AHEAD

* What was it like to write your own life story?
* Why did you include these specific memories?
* What did you leave out of your story? Why did you leave it out?
* What other details would you like to include?
* How has your story shaped who you are as a person today?
* How will your story shape who you become in the future?

LETTER TO MY FUTURE SELF

The future can seem like it's a long way off to kids, but imagining what's ahead of them can help kids set goals and achieve them while actively helping shape their identity. Help your child write a letter to their future self that encourages a focus on self-love.

Age Range:	**7–11**
Skills:	**Self-reflection**
Materials:	**Paper, pencil, envelope**
Number of Participants:	**1+**
Where to Play:	**Inside**

BEFORE YOU START

★ Talk about your child's hopes and dreams for the future. What do they imagine they'll be like? Share some of your own hopes and dreams for your future self, or tell your child what you imagined you'd be like as an adult.

HOW TO PLAY

★ Help your child write a letter to their future self. Encourage them to think about what they'll be doing in 5–10 years. What do they hope for themselves? Your child can use these sentence starters:
  • I hope I still like...
  • I hope I am friends with...
  • I hope I have achieved...
  • I hope I feel...
  • I hope I show myself love by...
★ Put the letter in an envelope and put it in a safe place. Save it for your child to open on a specific date.

THINKING BACK AND LOOKING AHEAD

★ What is it like to think about yourself in the future?
★ What do you think is most important for future you—achieving things or feeling loved? Why?
★ How can I help you remember that you are always worthy of love?

LIFE TIME LINE

In this activity, you'll help your child create a life time line to highlight the meaningful experiences in their life and create positive self-talk around hard times. Offering kind words to say to themselves around hard times will help your child remember that even though they can't always control what happens in life, they are still worthy of love, and their identity is secure regardless of what happens around them.

Age Range:	8–11
Skills:	Self-reflection, self-awareness, self-affirmation
Materials:	Paper, writing utensil, coloring utensils, photos and glue (optional), picture frame (optional)
Number of Participants:	1+
Where to Play:	Inside or virtually

BEFORE YOU START

★ Talk about what a time line is. You could say something like, "A time line is something that shows events that happened over time, in order. We can create time lines of our lives to show the events and memories we have experienced."

★ Talk about what an affirmation is. You can say, "An affirmation is a short, positive statement that can offer support and encouragement."

HOW TO PLAY

★ Help your child create a time line, starting with when they were born. (Some children may want to create it on a computer instead.)

★ Encourage your child to add all important events and both good and bad experiences.

★ Your child may choose to draw a symbol to go with each event, simply write the events, or add real photos for each event.

(continued on next page)

* Once the time line is complete, help your child create affirmations to go with each big event. It might look something like this:
  * Age 5:
    * Event: I tried gymnastics for the first time.
    * Affirmation: I can try new things!
  * Age 6:
    * Event: I broke my arm.
    * Affirmation: It's okay to take time to rest and heal my body.
  * Age 7:
    * Event: We moved from Georgia to California.
    * Affirmation: It's okay to feel sad.
* Hang the time line somewhere highly visible, or frame it for your child. You may also choose to add an extra sheet of paper to the end so they can continue to add on!

THINKING BACK AND LOOKING AHEAD

* What was it like to think about all your experiences?
* How did you feel when you included the positive or good experiences?
* How did you feel when you included the hard experiences?
* How do these affirmations change the way you think about these experiences?

MANDALA MAGIC

Mandalas are geometric arrangements of symbols that can bring focus, calmness, and peace. Help your child create a special mandala that represents their complete and whole identity. As they look at their beautiful design, kids will be reminded of the values, beliefs, and ideals that matter most to them, helping them solidify love and worth within their identity.

Age Range:	8–11
Skills:	Self-reflection, creativity
Materials:	Paper, pencil, coloring utensils (optional)
Number of Participants:	1+
Where to Play:	Inside

BEFORE YOU START

* Explain what a mandala is by saying something like, "The word 'mandala' is Sanskrit for 'circle.' A mandala is a symmetrical design with a central focal point. Mandalas are commonly found in Hindu and Buddhist cultures and are used in meditation and rituals."
* Look at some examples of mandalas by doing a quick search online or by looking at a mandala coloring book.
* Talk about ideals, beliefs, and values that are important to your child. Help them think about symbols that could represent these things. Prompt them with questions like:
  * What do you love to do?
  * What do you want to be known for?
  * What do you love most about yourself?
  * What do you love about your culture, religion, or community?

HOW TO PLAY

* Help your child sketch a design for a mandala. Start with a circle and add more symmetrical lines and shapes. Leave some open spaces inside the mandala.

(continued on next page)

* In the open spaces, help your child draw symbols to represent the ideals, beliefs, and values they chose to include. For example:
  * Loyalty: A heart
  * Heritage: A country flag
  * Love of music: Music notes or an instrument
* If desired, let your child add color to the mandala.
* Hang it somewhere highly visible so your child can see it often.

THINKING BACK AND LOOKING AHEAD
* Why did you choose these symbols and these values?
* How does your mandala represent you and your identity?
* How do you feel when you look at your mandala?
* How can your mandala help you feel grounded and connected to yourself?

PAST SELF

Comparing yourself to others can easily lead to negative feelings. Instead, help your child compare their current self to their past self rather than comparing themselves to others. Being able to see their own progress, rather than looking at other people's performance, will help them appreciate their own efforts and build a more loving perspective toward themselves.

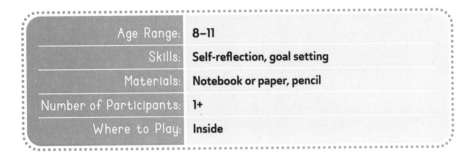

Age Range:	8–11
Skills:	Self-reflection, goal setting
Materials:	Notebook or paper, pencil
Number of Participants:	1+
Where to Play:	Inside

BEFORE YOU START

★ Identify a goal your child is working toward.

★ Talk about how we measure progress toward a goal. Do we measure our progress compared to others? Or to ourselves? Which one would be more beneficial for progress?

★ Talk about how comparing our progress to other people's can sometimes be motivating...but can sometimes be discouraging. You might add something like, "Other people have different experiences, different time, different tools, and different skills...and all of that impacts performance. If we compare ourselves to others, we aren't always comparing equal experiences. But if we compare ourselves to ourselves, we can truly see and measure growth!"

HOW TO PLAY

★ Have your child write their goal in a notebook or on a piece of paper.

★ Help your child keep track of what they can do right now. Have them write their current ability underneath the goal.

★ After a time interval—such as a week or month, depending on the activity or skill—have your child add an entry about what they can do right now.

(continued on next page)

* Help your child reflect on their current and past performance to see how they compare.
* Continue logging what they can do right now until they reach the goal they have set out to achieve. Here's an example:
  * My goal: I want to do a full 2-minute balance beam routine with a cartwheel without falling.
  * What I can do right now:
    * September 4: I can do about 20 seconds on the beam without falling.
    * September 12: I can do a 30-second routine on the beam with small jumps without falling.
    * September 29: I can do a 30-second routine with a cartwheel on the beam without falling.
    * October 4: I can do a 45-second routine with a cartwheel on the beam without falling.
    * October 15: I can do a 1-minute routine on the beam with no jumping without falling.
    * October 25: I can do a 1-minute routine on the beam with a cartwheel without falling.
    * November 13: I can do a 1-minute, 30-second routine on the beam with a cartwheel without falling.
    * November 27: I can do a 1-minute, 45-second routine on the beam with no flipping without falling.
    * December 15: I can do a 1-minute, 45-second routine on the beam with a cartwheel without falling.
    * January 5: I can do a 2-minute routine on the beam with no flipping without falling.
    * January 29: I can do a 2-minute routine on the beam with a cartwheel without falling!!!

THINKING BACK AND LOOKING AHEAD

* How did it feel when you first started your progress log?
* What is it like to see your growth over time?
* How do you feel when you compare yourself to your own progress?
* Were there any times when you wanted to compare yourself to others? How did that feel?
* How do you feel now that you have accomplished your goal?
* What other goals do you want to achieve now?

MEANINGFUL METAPHOR

Describing yourself can feel uncomfortable at first. Using metaphors can be a fun and creative way for kids to recognize their strengths. The more they focus on their great qualities, the more self-love kids will enjoy.

Age Range:	**8–11**
Skills:	**Self-reflection, creativity, communication**
Materials:	**Paper, pencil, coloring utensils**
Number of Participants:	**1+**
Where to Play:	**Inside**

BEFORE YOU START

★ Talk about what a metaphor is. You might say something like, "A metaphor is a figure of speech that describes something as another thing to help make a comparison. A metaphor says that one thing is another thing using symbolism to show their connection."

★ Look at some examples of metaphors, like:
- Life is a highway.
- Her tears are a river.
- His room is a pigsty.
- The classroom is a zoo.

HOW TO PLAY

★ Help your child think about a metaphor for themselves. What items, things, places, or landforms could describe them? They might come up with something like:
- She is a tall and strong mountain.
- He is a shining star.
- They are an artistic masterpiece.

★ Have your child write the metaphor on the top of a piece of paper.

(continued on next page)

* Have your child illustrate the metaphor. They might draw themselves as the thing they used to describe themselves in the metaphor. For example, your child could draw her face on a tall and strong mountain.
* Display the metaphor and artwork somewhere highly visible so your child can see it often.

THINKING BACK AND LOOKING AHEAD
* What is it like to think about yourself as this thing?
* Why did you pick this thing? What qualities or characteristics do you share with it?
* How does it feel to look at your metaphor artwork? What does it remind you of?
* How will you feel when you look at it in the future?

FOUR SQUARE

Identity is both internal and external. In this activity, kids will think about how they see themselves, how others see them, and how they might like any of those views to change. Self-reflection on who they are and who they'd like to be will help kids solidify their sense of identity and plan for how to let that identity show to others. This whole process will help kids think lovingly about themselves and their identities.

Age Range:	**8–11**
Skills:	**Self-reflection**
Materials:	**Paper, writing utensil**
Number of Participants:	**1+**
Where to Play:	**Inside or virtually**

BEFORE YOU START

* Talk about how your child sees themselves. What qualities do they see in themselves? Is there anything they'd like to change or improve on?
* Talk about how sometimes other people see us differently than we see ourselves. Discuss why this might happen. We might act a certain way, say certain things, or make choices that give other people a perception or view about us and who we are. This might not always match how we see ourselves, because we may want others to see us differently.
* Talk about how your child thinks other people view them. You can use specific examples like:
  * How do you think Grandma sees you?
  * How do you think your teacher sees you?
  * How do you think your friends see you?

(continued on next page)

HOW TO PLAY

* Divide a piece of paper into four sections. (Or, a child could create this on a computer.) Label the sections:
  * How I See Me
  * How I Think Others See Me
  * How I Want to See Me
  * How I Want Others to See Me
* In each section, have your child write each viewpoint as they currently see it. Here's an example:

How I See Me	How I Think Others See Me
Thoughtful, sensitive, kind, stressed	Successful, hard worker, smart
How I Want to See Me	**How I Want Others to See Me**
Thoughtful, sensitive, kind, brave, relaxed	Successful, hard worker, smart, kind, needs help sometimes

* Talk about what they included and why.
* If there are differences in the ways they see themselves and how they want to see themselves or in the ways they think others see them and how they want others to see them, talk about what steps they could take to make these more aligned.

THINKING BACK AND LOOKING AHEAD

* Why do you think there are differences in how you see yourself and how others see you?
* Are there any ways I can help you take steps to see yourself the way you'd like to?
* Are there any ways I can help you show others you have the qualities you'd like them to see in you?

TIME CAPSULE

Time capsules are fun to make and even more fun to open at a later date. Help your child create a time capsule that represents who they are. Spending time carefully choosing items to include will help your child engage in self-reflection about their identity. Choosing special items that represent them will help them feel lovingly toward themselves.

Age Range:	8–11
Skills:	Self-reflection
Materials:	Sealable container, contents for time capsule (chosen by child)
Number of Participants:	1+
Where to Play:	Inside

BEFORE YOU START

* Talk about what a time capsule is. You could say something like, "Time capsules are things that people make to share a part of themselves and a part of history with people in the future or with their future selves. They are a reminder of what was important to a person in the past."
* Talk about what they might like to remember about themselves as they are right now. How might they be able to represent who they are and what they like right now?

HOW TO PLAY

* Choose a container for your time capsule.
* Choose a date to open the time capsule, and write it on the top of the container. For example, you might choose their high school graduation date or a milestone birthday.

(continued on next page)

* Help your child gather items to include in the time capsule. They might want to include things such as:
  * Family pictures
  * Artwork
  * A newspaper clipping from an achievement
  * A picture or drawing of their favorite toy or stuffed animal
  * A list of favorite songs
  * A letter to their future self
* Place the items in the time capsule, seal it, and put it away until the date it will be opened.

THINKING BACK AND LOOKING AHEAD

* What was it like to choose items for your time capsule?
* What does each item represent about who you are and your identity?
* What do you think it will be like to open this in the future? How do you think you will feel? Do you think you will have similar interests and qualities?

CHAPTER 9

WORTH

WHAT IS WORTH?

A sense of self-worth is a feeling of deserving good things, belonging with others, and deserving love. A sense of self-worth is associated with an overall positive opinion of oneself and nonjudgment, acceptance, and gentleness toward oneself. Self-worth is different from self-esteem in that while self-esteem can be drawn from external influences, achievements, and successes, self-worth comes from within and relies only on internal feelings. Showing unconditional love, positive regard, and respect and giving kids a chance to experience success are some ways that caregivers can help kids build self-worth.

HOW DOES WORTH RELATE TO SELF-LOVE?

Kids with strong self-worth value themselves and believe they are worthy of love and good treatment. As they develop a sense of self-worth, they rely less on external encouragement or praise and derive love and value from internal feelings. Kids who feel worthy believe they deserve to be treated with respect. When kids believe they are worthy of good things, they are more likely to accept and love themselves just as they are.

WHAT DOES WORTH LOOK AND SOUND LIKE?

The outward demonstration of a feeling of worth involves treating yourself well and with care and expecting the same from others. Some examples of outward demonstrations of worth include:

* Taking care of your physical, mental, emotional, social, and spiritual needs
* Setting appropriate boundaries
* Expecting fair, kind, and respectful treatment from others
* Being compassionate and forgiving toward yourself

WORTH IN KID-FRIENDLY TERMS

To explain worth to your kid, try saying something like this:

> *What are some things that are worth a lot? Big toys, houses, gold? You are worth a lot too! Knowing that you have worth and value means that you know you deserve to be treated well and taken care of. Knowing you have worth also means that you do things to take care of yourself, show yourself love, and be gentle and kind to yourself.*

LOOKING AHEAD

In this chapter, you'll find activities that encourage kids to explore exactly how they value themselves. You'll also find activities that inspire kids to show themselves how they are valued on a regular basis.

LOVE PRINT

High five for self-love! This activity will help kids identify five things they love about themselves as a reminder of the worth they have and the love they have to give themselves. They can use this visual anytime, anywhere to quickly access these positive feelings.

Age Range:	5–7
Skills:	Creativity, self-awareness
Materials:	Paper, coloring utensils
Number of Participants:	1+
Where to Play:	Inside

BEFORE YOU START

★ Talk about qualities your child might love about themselves (focusing on internal qualities over appearances). You can model this for your child by sharing what you love about yourself. Remind them of the things you love most about them as well.

HOW TO PLAY

★ On paper, help your child trace their hand.
★ Inside each finger outline, help your child write a reason they love themselves. There will be five reasons altogether.
★ Hang the handprint somewhere highly visible.
★ Encourage your child to give the handprint a high five each day and say the five things they love about themselves!

THINKING BACK AND LOOKING AHEAD

★ How does it feel to give yourself a high five?
★ How does it feel to say the reasons you love yourself out loud?
★ How will these high fives help you throughout the day?

FACES OF ME

Sometimes, kids get the message that feelings like anger, frustration, and sadness are not okay. But *all* feelings are a part of life and offer important information about the way we experience the world. Take photos of your child showing a range of emotions and make a collage to remind them that all feelings are okay to experience. Accepting their emotions as a part of life will remind kids that they, and their feelings, are worthy of love and attention.

Age Range:	**5–8**
Skills:	**Self-awareness**
Materials:	**Camera, photo collage app on phone or computer, printer, picture frame (optional)**
Number of Participants:	**1+**
Where to Play:	**Inside or virtually**

BEFORE YOU START

★ Make a list of feelings. Ask your child if they think any of these are "good" or "bad" feelings.

★ Talk about how all feelings are okay and none are good or bad. You could say something like, "All feelings are a part of life and okay to experience. What we do with our feelings matters. Recognizing how we feel and then choosing positive ways to acknowledge, honor, and manage our feelings is a way to show ourselves love."

HOW TO PLAY

★ Take photos of your child showing faces and body language of different emotions, like:

- Happy
- Sad
- Angry
- Worried

- Excited
- Scared
- Frustrated
- Confused

- Lonely
- Bored
- Silly

★ Use a photo collage app on your phone or computer to make a collage of the pictures. Add labels to name the feelings.

★ Print the collage, and hang it somewhere highly visible or frame it.

* When your child has big feelings, ask them to use the collage as a reference point to name their emotion using this formula:
  * I feel _____, and that feeling is okay. I can _____ to help myself feel better/experience this feeling/be okay.
* For example, your child might say:
  * "I feel angry, and that feeling is okay. I can take deep breaths to help myself feel better."
  * "I feel worried, and that feeling is okay. I can ask for help to be okay."
  * "I feel happy, and that feeling is okay. I can write about it in my journal to experience this feeling."
* Remind your child that all feelings are okay and worthy of attention and love! They can show themselves love by honoring and acknowledging their feelings.

THINKING BACK AND LOOKING AHEAD

* How does it feel to name your feelings?
* How does it feel to do things to take care of your feelings?
* How can I remind you that all your feelings are okay?

AFFIRMATION HOPSCOTCH

An affirmation is a short, positive statement that can offer support and encouragement. This activity combines hopscotch with affirmations your child can say to themselves to blend fun movement with affirming self-love.

Age Range:	**5–9**
Skills:	**Self-affirmation, creativity**
Materials:	**Chalk, beanbag or small rock**
Number of Participants:	**1+**
Where to Play:	**Outside**

BEFORE YOU START

★ Talk about what an affirmation is. You could say something like, "An affirmation is a statement or sentence that we say to ourselves to build ourselves up, encourage ourselves, or remind ourselves of strengths and values. Saying or reading affirmations can make us feel good about ourselves, and affirmations can help us focus on the good within ourselves, especially when things feel hard or challenging."

HOW TO PLAY

★ On the sidewalk or driveway, draw a hopscotch path with your child.
★ Inside each space of the hopscotch path, write affirmations for your child to say. It might look something like the image on the facing page.
★ Your child will stand on the start of the hopscotch path. They will toss the beanbag or rock and hop to the space where it lands. As they hop along, they will say the affirmations that are in the boxes they are stepping in.

THINKING BACK AND LOOKING AHEAD

★ How did it feel to say these affirmations out loud?
★ Which one is your favorite?
★ What other times of day could you say these to yourself?

FINISH

I am
awesome!

My unique-
ness makes
the world
better.

I believe
in myself.

I can be
kind to
myself.

I have
good
ideas.

I matter.

I am
loved.

START

BEADS OF LOVE

We all need a little reminder of the good in life sometimes! Pick up some colorful beads and string to make self-love bracelets or bookmarks. Each color will be a gentle reminder to your child of the things they love about themselves each time they look at it.

Age Range:	5–11
Skills:	Creativity, enthusiasm, admiration
Materials:	Colorful beads, paper, writing utensil, string or pipe cleaner
Number of Participants:	1+
Where to Play:	Inside

BEFORE YOU START
★ Talk about qualities your child loves about themselves (focusing on internal qualities over appearances). You can model this for your child by sharing what you love about yourself. Remind them of the things you love most about them as well.

HOW TO PLAY
★ Sort your beads by color.
★ With your child, write down a list of things they love about themselves. Turn these into self-love statements to make them extra powerful. For example, "I love my curiosity," or "I love my kindness." For younger children, you might want to provide them with self-love statements to start.
★ Assign each self-love statement to a color bead (e.g., green = I love my curiosity, blue = I love my kindness).
★ Place the beads on the string or pipe cleaner.
★ Tie the string or pipe cleaner into a bracelet, or tie the ends to make a bookmark.
★ Practice repeating the self-love statements when pointing to each color.
★ This can become a part of your child's daily routine. In the morning, have your child point to one or all of the beads and repeat the self-love

statements as a way to start the day. Or this can be used in difficult moments when your child needs a reminder of their worth.

* How will you feel when you look at the beads on your bracelet/ bookmark?
* Which one of these beads is most important to you?
* In what ways can I remind you of these things when you're having a hard day?

As they repeat these statements, the statements will move from external dialogue to internal thoughts, becoming a part of your child's important self-talk. The more they practice, the more naturally this self-talk will come to them in hard moments.

PERSONAL VALENTINE

Be your own valentine! Receiving love from others feels good, but kids should also learn that it's important to give love to themselves. Creating a valentine for themselves will remind them that they are worthy of love.

Age Range:	**5–11**
Skills:	**Creativity, self-reflection**
Materials:	**Paper or construction paper, scissors, coloring utensils, art supplies, pencil, picture frame (optional)**
Number of Participants:	**1+**
Where to Play:	**Inside**

BEFORE YOU START

★ Talk about what a valentine is if your child is not yet familiar. You can say something like, "A valentine is a card or letter that someone gives another person to tell them that they care about them. You can also give yourself a valentine as a reminder that you love yourself."

HOW TO PLAY

★ Using paper or construction paper, create a valentine. Let your child be as creative as they want with this. Cut the paper into hearts, draw hearts, or design anything else they'd like to make. Add stickers, glitter, or any other details your child wants.

★ Inside the card that they make for themselves, have your child write a love note to themselves. Younger children might need help with the writing. It might look something like this:

  • Dear Me, I love you! You have a lot of amazing qualities that make the world a better place! Always remember that. Love, Me.

★ Place the valentine somewhere highly visible where your child will see it often, or frame it!

THINKING BACK AND LOOKING AHEAD

★ How did it feel to make a valentine for yourself?
★ What would it be like if you told yourself that you love yourself each day?

I FEEL LOVED WHEN...

We all experience and feel love in different ways, and children are no different. Help your child identify ways that they feel loved by others and then brainstorm ways they could show themselves love in these same ways. Talking about the ways they feel loved will remind them that they are loved and that they deserve love!

Age Range:	**5–11**
Skills:	**Self-reflection**
Materials:	**Paper, writing utensil, coloring utensils (optional)**
Number of Participants:	**1+**
Where to Play:	**Inside**

BEFORE YOU START

★ Talk about different ways that we can show people love. This could look like:
- Saying, "I love you."
- Helping someone.
- Sitting with someone when they are having a hard day.
- Giving someone a hug.
- Making food for someone.
- Giving someone a small gift.

HOW TO PLAY

★ Ask your child to think about the times when they feel loved.
★ Together on paper, make a list of the ways your child feels loved. You can also let your child draw pictures of how they feel loved.
★ It might look something like this: I feel loved when...
- Dad rubs my back when I fall asleep.
- Mom brings me a snow globe from her business trips.
- Grandma takes me to the lake to feed the ducks.
- Grandpa gives me a big, spinning hug.

(continued on next page)

* If your child's list includes only ways that other people show them love, ask them to include a few ways they show themselves love. They might include things like:
  * I spend some alone time in my room writing in my journal.
  * I paint a picture of the places I love.

THINKING BACK AND LOOKING AHEAD
* What is it like to think about the ways you feel loved?
* Do you often think about how you can show yourself love too?
* In what other ways could you show yourself love?
* How can I make sure that I'm showing you love often?

I AM... DAY

How many positive traits do you have already? Let's find out! In this activity, encourage your child to recognize ways they demonstrate positive traits and highlight all the good things about them. Taking time to celebrate their own positive traits will help kids see the good in themselves.

Age Range:	5–11
Skills:	Creativity, self-reflection
Materials:	Paper or notebook, coloring utensils or pencil (optional)
Number of Participants:	1+
Where to Play:	Inside

BEFORE YOU START

* Make or find online a list of positive adjectives or character traits.

HOW TO PLAY

* Choose a positive adjective for the day or week.
* Throughout the day or week, encourage your child to state examples, draw pictures, or write in a journal about ways they possess or demonstrate that positive adjective. If your child wants to keep a journal for this activity, write the positive trait on the top of a page in a notebook. They can list or draw their examples on the page.
* Set a goal for how many examples they should come up with. Start with a low number and gradually increase it as you continue this activity or as your child gets older.
* Here's an example: This week, tell or draw five examples of how you are generous.
  1. I share my books with my sister.
  2. I give away toys I don't play with anymore.
  3. I share my snack with a friend when they don't have a snack.
  4. I collected cans for the food drive at school.
  5. I helped make dinner for Mrs. Yamashiro when she had surgery.

(continued on next page)

★ If your child is having trouble coming up with examples of ways they already demonstrate or possess this positive trait, help them make a list of ways they *could* demonstrate it!

THINKING BACK AND LOOKING AHEAD

★ What was it like to think about yourself as [this positive trait]?

★ Did you know before we did this that you possessed this trait?

★ Are you surprised by how many positive traits you have already?

★ What other positive traits would you like to work on?

Here is a list of positive traits you can use for this exercise:

- Generous
- Peaceful
- Encouraging
- Supportive
- Fun
- Friendly
- Helpful
- Hardworking

3-2-1 DINNER REFLECTION

Self-reflection is important for growth, and so is support from loved ones. Spending time during dinner (or other family time) to reflect on the day can give your child an opportunity to recognize the things they did well and things they might need help with. This practice encourages kids to see themselves as worthy of love and support and offer themselves some compassion as they learn and grow.

Age Range:	6–11
Skills:	Self-reflection
Materials:	Paper, printer or writing utensil, lamination machine or picture frame (optional)
Number of Participants:	The whole family
Where to Play:	Inside

BEFORE YOU START

★ Create a simple visual on a piece of paper that everyone can reference as they share about their days. Type it up and print it, or write it on paper, and laminate or frame it for longevity so you can use it as a conversation guide for weeks and years to come. Your self-reflection questions can be these, or you can create your own:
  - 3: Share 3 things you did well today.
  - 2: Share 2 new things you tried today.
  - 1: Share 1 challenge you faced today.

HOW TO PLAY

★ During dinner or daily family time, offer everyone time to share their 3-2-1 reflection statements.

★ You can go around in a circle, where everyone shares their 3s, then everyone shares their 2s, and then their 1s, or one person can share all things at once before moving to the next person.

★ When each person shares their challenge, they can also say whether or not they'd like help with the challenge. If they'd like help, others in the family can offer advice or encouragement.

(continued on next page)

THINKING BACK AND LOOKING AHEAD

* What is it like to share these things each day?
* How does sharing what you did well change the way you think and feel about yourself?
* How does sharing your challenges with everyone feel?
* How does it feel to hear what others are doing well and the challenges others have?
* How can we use this time to encourage each other to be more loving toward ourselves?

AFFIRMATION JAR

An affirmation is a short, positive statement that can offer support and encouragement. We all need affirmations from time to time! In this activity, kids will grab a jar, some colorful paper, and their favorite pens and create an affirmation jar. This will give kids an easy way to quickly grab a reminder of all the ways they are worthy of love.

Age Range:	7–11
Skills:	Creativity, enthusiasm, admiration
Materials:	Strips of colored paper; pens or markers; jar; paint markers, stickers, or gems (optional)
Number of Participants:	1+
Where to Play:	Inside

BEFORE YOU START

★ Talk about what an affirmation is. You could say something like, "An affirmation is a statement or sentence that we say to ourselves to build ourselves up, encourage ourselves, or remind ourselves of strengths and values. Saying or reading affirmations can make us feel good about ourselves, and affirmations can help us focus on the good within ourselves, especially when things feel hard or challenging."

HOW TO PLAY

★ On strips of paper, write affirmations with your child. Here are some examples:
  • I am enough.
  • I am amazingly me.
  • I have special gifts to share with the world.
  • I am loved.
★ Place all the affirmations in the jar.
★ If you want, decorate the jar with paint markers, stickers, or gems.
★ Place the jar in a highly visible place or a place where your child will see it often and can access it themselves.

(continued on next page)

* When your child needs an affirmation, they can pick one from the jar to read silently or aloud, take with them for the day, place in their pocket, or use in any other way that's helpful.
* You may want to designate a specific time of the week to get an affirmation, like first thing Monday morning, to make it a routine for your child.

THINKING BACK AND LOOKING AHEAD
* How does it feel to read this affirmation?
* How will this affirmation encourage you today/this week?
* What does this affirmation remind you about yourself or your worth?

POSITIVE WORD OF THE WEEK

Mindset shifts can make a big difference! Help your child shift their own mindset by building a positive vocabulary. Give them positive words to work into everyday conversation to direct their thoughts toward positive things. When they see the world and others in a more positive light, they'll start to see and treat themselves in a more positive light too.

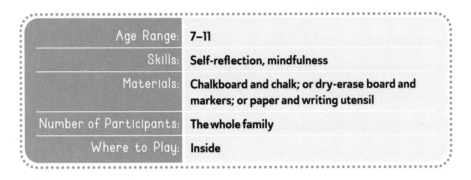

Age Range:	**7–11**
Skills:	**Self-reflection, mindfulness**
Materials:	**Chalkboard and chalk; or dry-erase board and markers; or paper and writing utensil**
Number of Participants:	**The whole family**
Where to Play:	**Inside**

BEFORE YOU START

* Make a list of positive words you'd like your child to know and use.
* Talk about how our thoughts, feelings, and actions are all related. When we take positive actions, including using positive words, we think more positive thoughts, and we feel more positive feelings.

HOW TO PLAY

* Each week, choose one positive word for the family. Write it on a family chalkboard or dry-erase board, or just write it on paper and hang it on the refrigerator.
* Challenge family members to use the positive word to describe others, describe the world or community, and describe themselves as often as possible throughout the week.
* This can be a daily practice at a specific time of day, like dinnertime, or it can be a more fluid activity that children do in their own timing.

(continued on next page)

THINKING BACK AND LOOKING AHEAD

★ What is it like to describe others positively? The community? Yourself?

★ How do you feel when you use positive words?

★ What actions did you want to take as a result of this positive word?

★ What other positive words should we include in this practice?

....

Here's a list of positive words to get you started:

• Beautiful

• Generous

• Kind

• Peaceful

• Inclusive

• Genuine

• Brilliant

• Enchanting

• Motivating/motivated

• Impressive

....

MIRROR AFFIRMATIONS

Mirror, mirror on the wall, who's as worthy as them all? Everyone! In this activity, kids will write affirmations on sticky notes and stick them to a mirror for daily reminders of their worth.

Age Range:	**7–11**
Skills:	**Self-affirmation**
Materials:	**Sticky notes, writing utensil**
Number of Participants:	**1+**
Where to Play:	**Inside**

BEFORE YOU START
* Talk about the importance of a positive start to the day. You might talk about how starting the day with positivity can change the way you look at things throughout the day. It can change the way you interact with others, and it can change the way you think and feel about yourself.

HOW TO PLAY
* Brainstorm affirmations with your child. On sticky notes, write your child's favorites. You may want to spend time together looking up affirmations online, then let your child choose the ones they like best.
* Stick the affirmations around the border of a mirror in the child's bedroom or the bathroom they use most.
* Each day, help your child develop a routine of reading and saying aloud two or three of the affirmations while looking in the mirror.

THINKING BACK AND LOOKING AHEAD
* Which affirmations are your favorite?
* Which affirmations will be most meaningful to you when you read them?
* How do you think starting your day with these affirmations will change your day?

AFFIRMATION BUBBLE ART

Help your child create an artistic representation of a protective bubble they can create in their minds to show themselves some love and remember their worth when hard times arise. Kids will think of affirmations to remind themselves of their worth during tough situations so they have them on hand in difficult moments.

Age Range:	**8–11**
Skills:	**Self-care, creativity, self-affirmation**
Materials:	**Paper; pencil; watercolor paints and paintbrushes, or other coloring utensils; picture frame (optional)**
Number of Participants:	**1+**
Where to Play:	**Inside**

BEFORE YOU START

* Talk about experiences, words, or messages your child faces that can make them question their worth or feel bad. Offer some examples from your own life or own past experiences.
* Talk about how we can help ourselves remember our worth by reciting affirmations. These are words we say to build ourselves up and remind ourselves of what we believe to be true about ourselves.

HOW TO PLAY

* In the middle of a piece of paper, have your child draw themselves.
* Have your child draw a large circle or bubble around themselves, leaving space to write inside and outside the bubble.
* Outside the bubble, have your child write experiences or words that are hard for them and can cause them to question their worth. They might write things like:
  * When people make fun of me
  * When I get bad grades
  * When I feel left out

* Inside the circle, have your child write affirmations they can say to themselves to remind themselves of their worth. They might write things like:
  * I love who I am.
  * I can keep trying.
  * I matter.
  * I deserve love.
* Let your child color or use watercolors to paint the picture. They can paint themselves and then use different colors to differentiate between the bubble and the outside messages.
* Hang this somewhere highly visible or frame it for your child to see often.

THINKING BACK AND LOOKING AHEAD

* What was it like to think about the things that can bring you down (outside the bubble)? What feelings do you have?
* What was it like to write these affirmations to yourself (inside the bubble)? What feelings do you have?
* What is it like to imagine a protective bubble around yourself?
* How can you use these affirmations when things feel hard?
* How can I help you remember your worth when things feel hard?

POSITIVE EXPERIENCES NOTEBOOK

Sometimes it can be hard for kids to focus on the small, good things in life—a single tough experience can claim their attention instead. In this activity, kids will jot down small, positive experiences from the day to highlight the good things. Focusing on even the smallest good things can serve as a great reminder of not only the good around us but the good within us as well.

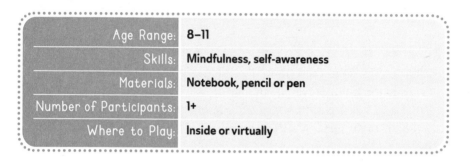

Age Range:	**8–11**
Skills:	**Mindfulness, self-awareness**
Materials:	**Notebook, pencil or pen**
Number of Participants:	**1+**
Where to Play:	**Inside or virtually**

BEFORE YOU START

★ Talk about positive experiences and what they might feel like. You could say something like, "Positive experiences are things we notice, see, hear, taste, or feel throughout the day that leave us feeling good, happy, fulfilled, valued, worthy, or close to others."

★ Give some examples. Positive experiences can be things like:
- Spending time with a friend
- Reading a heartwarming story
- Seeing a cute video of a puppy
- Being complimented by someone
- Helping someone
- Seeing a stranger do something kind for someone
- Overcoming a challenge
- Having fun while trying something new
- Enjoying a new food
- Seeing beautiful flowers or trees
- Going to a new playground

HOW TO PLAY

* Choose a notebook and pencil or pen that your child likes. Or, make a document your child can write in on a computer.
* Each day, sit with your child and encourage them to write or draw about at least one positive experience they had during the day. It could be something big, like being recognized in front of their whole class for an achievement. Or it could be something small, like noticing wildflowers growing through the sidewalk.
* If your child is comfortable sharing their positive experience, talk about it together and reflect on the good things from the day, big or small. Share your own too!

THINKING BACK AND LOOKING AHEAD

* What's it like to think about your positive experiences today?
* Is it easy or hard to think of something that was positive?
* How do you think taking time to notice these positive things changes your day?
* What positive experiences do you want to have tomorrow? What steps can you take to make them happen?

SELF-FORGIVENESS EXERCISE

We all deserve love and forgiveness, but sometimes it can be hard for kids to forgive themselves for things they've done or said. Spend time practicing self-forgiveness to remind kids that no matter what has happened in the past, they are still worthy of love from others and from themselves.

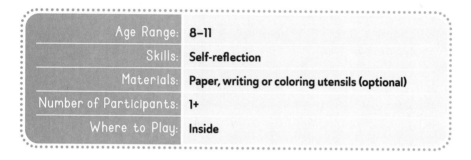

Age Range:	**8–11**
Skills:	**Self-reflection**
Materials:	**Paper, writing or coloring utensils (optional)**
Number of Participants:	**1+**
Where to Play:	**Inside**

BEFORE YOU START

★ Talk about what "forgiveness" means. You could say something like, "'Forgiveness' means we let go of something, do not hold on to bad feelings about an experience, and move on while showing compassion. We can forgive others when they hurt us with their bodies, words, or actions. And we can also forgive ourselves when we make mistakes."

HOW TO PLAY

★ Talk with your child about an experience or action they are having trouble letting go of, in which they made a mistake, hurt someone, or hurt themselves. It could be something like:
  • I broke my favorite toy.
  • I said some things that hurt my best friend's feelings.
  • I lied to my mom.
★ Your child can draw a picture of the event, write about the event, or simply share the experience verbally.
★ If your child drew or wrote about the experience, you can have them tear up the paper over the recycling bin and say, "We all make mistakes. I deserve forgiveness. I forgive myself because I love myself." If your child shared the experience verbally, they can simply say this affirmation.

THINKING BACK AND LOOKING AHEAD

* What was it like to think about this mistake/experience again?
* What feelings did you have when you tore the paper/said the affirmation?
* How does it feel to forgive yourself?
* How can you remind yourself that you deserve forgiveness? How can I help remind you?

SELF-LOVE FORTUNE-TELLER

What's your fortune? Self-worth affirmations! Make a paper fortune-teller with your child's favorite affirmations to remind them of their beauty and worth.

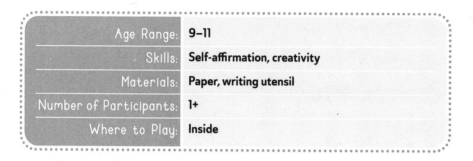

Age Range:	**9–11**
Skills:	**Self-affirmation, creativity**
Materials:	**Paper, writing utensil**
Number of Participants:	**1+**
Where to Play:	**Inside**

BEFORE YOU START

★ Talk about what an affirmation is. You could say something like, "An affirmation is a statement or sentence that we say to ourselves to build ourselves up, encourage ourselves, or remind ourselves of strengths and values. Saying or reading affirmations can make us feel good about ourselves, and affirmations can help us focus on the good within ourselves, especially when things feel hard or challenging."

HOW TO PLAY

★ Use paper to make a folded fortune-teller. There are lots of templates online if you aren't sure how to do this.
★ Fill in the fortune-teller:
  • On the outside corners, write color words.
  • On the outside triangles, write numbers.
  • On the inside triangles, write affirmations that your child loves.

★ Here's an example:

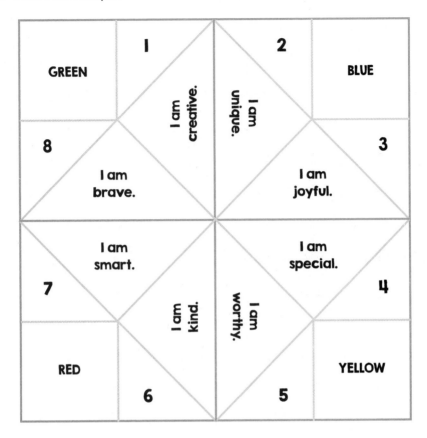

★ Fold the fortune-teller.
★ Have your child choose a color. Spell the color while opening and closing the fortune-teller.
★ Have your child choose a number. Open and close the fortune-teller while counting to that number.
★ Have them choose another number. Open the flap and read the affirmation.

THINKING BACK AND LOOKING AHEAD
★ Why did you choose these affirmations?
★ How does it feel to read them?
★ When will you use these affirmations to help you?

PERSONAL COMPLIMENTS JOURNAL

It's always nice to receive compliments from others, but kids should know that they can also pay themselves compliments. Help your child develop this practice using a daily journal. Setting aside time for reflection and gentleness will encourage your child to see themselves in a positive light and offer themselves the love they are so worthy of!

Age Range:	**9–11**
Skills:	**Self-reflection**
Materials:	**Physical or digital journal, writing utensil (if using physical journal), coloring utensils (optional)**
Number of Participants:	**1+**
Where to Play:	**Inside or virtually**

BEFORE YOU START

* Get a physical or digital journal for your child.
* Talk about what a compliment is. You could say something like, "A compliment is something we say to let someone know that we recognize something positive about them. It could be that we notice they did something well; we appreciate something they did; we like the way they dress, speak, sing, or paint; or something else! Compliments are best when they are specific, meaningful, and about skills or actions over appearances."
* Offer some examples. Genuine compliments can sound something like this:
  * I love the way you painted that landscape! I can really see the movement of the water.
  * I noticed that you are really kind to others. You're always going out of your way to make others feel good.
  * Wow, your flute song is really coming along! I can tell you have been working really hard on it.

HOW TO PLAY

* Give your child a journal.
* Set aside time each day for your child to write one compliment to themselves in the journal, such as after school, before dinner, or before bed. This might sound something like this:
  * Dear Self, you tried really hard in math today. Don't give up.
  * Dear Me, you were really kind to the kids in your class at recess. You included everyone.
  * I am a really hard worker. I tried my best today.
* If your child wants to, they can draw a picture to accompany the compliment.
* Set aside time to look over it together. You can do this each day or set aside time on the weekend to review all their self-compliments from the week.

THINKING BACK AND LOOKING AHEAD

* How does it feel to give yourself a compliment?
* What do you think is more meaningful to you—a compliment from others or a compliment to yourself? Why?
* What is it like to read back through these compliments?
* How can this journal help or encourage you in the future?

CHAPTER 10

PHYSICAL WELL-BEING

WHAT IS PHYSICAL WELL-BEING?

Physical well-being involves making balanced choices to promote a healthy lifestyle. It's not just about eating healthy and exercising; it's about making choices that promote a healthy view of oneself and the amazing things the body can do. When you help kids find activities they enjoy that support their body and mind, you are fostering an environment that can lead to self-love.

HOW DOES PHYSICAL WELL-BEING RELATE TO SELF-LOVE?

There is much written on the relationship between body image and self-esteem. Body image, or the way that you view and feel about your body, is different from physical well-being, though. While body image relates to the thoughts and feelings one has about their body, physical well-being refers more to the state of healthiness of the mind and body.

Developing healthy physical well-being is an act of self-love. We can help kids learn that taking care of their bodies and minds is a way to show themselves love. When we love ourselves, we make choices that take care of our bodies and minds.

WHAT DOES PHYSICAL WELL-BEING LOOK AND SOUND LIKE?

The outward demonstration of developing physical well-being involves actively seeking balance in activities, foods, etc. Some examples of outward demonstrations of physical well-being include:

* Trying a variety of physical activities to find enjoyed forms of movement
* Balancing time spent in activity and rest
* Choosing nourishing foods

- Seeing food as a way to fuel and nourish the body
- Seeing movement and exercise as a celebration of what the body can do
- Getting enough rest
- Engaging in appropriate hygiene activities
- Talking about and regulating emotions

PHYSICAL WELL-BEING IN KID-FRIENDLY TERMS

To explain physical well-being to your kids, try saying something like this:

There are lots of ways that we can take care of our bodies. We can eat delicious, nourishing foods; we can spend time moving our bodies; and we can get enough rest. But it's also important to take care of our minds! We can spend time talking about our feelings, take time to calm down when we need to, write in a journal, or say kind things to ourselves. Having physical well-being means that we are taking good care of our bodies and our minds.

LOOKING AHEAD

In this chapter, you'll find activities that encourage healthy choices for mind and body. You'll also find activities that encourage kids to try new things, make a plan for physical well-being success, and create healthy routines that support mind and body.

BODY OUTLINE AFFIRMATIONS

Kids should know that their bodies do amazing things! This exercise will help them reflect on all the things their bodies help them do to give themselves a self-love boost.

Age Range:	**5–7**
Skills:	**Self-reflection, creativity, gratitude**
Materials:	**Large paper and markers, or sidewalk chalk**
Number of Participants:	**1+**
Where to Play:	**Inside or outside**

BEFORE YOU START

★ Talk about all the amazing things your body helps you do. You might say things like:
  • My legs help me run, jump, skip, and kick a soccer ball!
  • My hands help me draw cartoon characters and make cool clay sculptures!
  • My brain helps me come up with new ideas and solve problems!

HOW TO PLAY

★ On a large piece of paper or on the sidewalk, trace the outline of your child's body.
★ Inside the body outline, help your child write reasons why they are grateful for their body.
★ Take a picture of your child with their body outline to save.

THINKING BACK AND LOOKING AHEAD

★ What is it like to focus on all the amazing things your body can do?
★ What do you think your life would be like if you took time every day to be grateful for your body?
★ How can I help you remember all the amazing things your body can do?

SELF-LOVE CATERPILLAR

Self-love should keep growing! Help your child create a visual display of their self-love by making a caterpillar. Each circle of the body will be a visual representation of one thing they love about their body.

Age Range:	**5–8**
Skills:	**Creativity, self-reflection**
Materials:	**Construction paper, scissors, bowl or cup, printer, glue, poster board, writing utensil**
Number of Participants:	**1+**
Where to Play:	**Inside**

BEFORE YOU START

★ Cut out circles from construction paper. Place them in a bowl or cup.
★ Cut out a bigger circle for the caterpillar head. Print a picture of your child and glue it on the caterpillar head. Add antennae if you want!
★ Glue the caterpillar head onto the left side of the poster board.

HOW TO PLAY

★ When your child notices or says something they like or appreciate about their body, help them write it on one of the circles. Then let your child glue it onto the poster board to build the caterpillar body.
★ The growing caterpillar will be a visual display of your child's growing self-love for their body!

THINKING BACK AND LOOKING AHEAD

★ How does it feel when you add a circle to the caterpillar?
★ What do you notice about your caterpillar compared to last week/ month/year?
★ What do you think it will look like next week/month/year?

BODY APPRECIATION

In this activity, kids will take a moment to appreciate all the things their bodies can do. Adopting this mindset allows them to build a healthy self-image, which will give them a greater overall sense of love for themselves.

Age Range:	**5–11**
Skills:	**Self-reflection, kindness**
Materials:	**Mirror**
Number of Participants:	**1+**
Where to Play:	**Anywhere with a tall mirror**

BEFORE YOU START

* Talk about what it means to appreciate your body. This may feel unnatural or uncomfortable to some kids. Model what it looks and sounds like for them! Here are some examples:
  * I appreciate my strong legs because they allow me to run and play tennis.
  * I appreciate my hands because they allow me to squeeze Play-Doh and pick flowers.
  * I appreciate my brain because it allows me to be curious and use my imagination.

HOW TO PLAY

* Have your child stand in front of a mirror.
* As they look at their reflection, have your child come up with at least three things they appreciate about their body.
* End the activity by having your child say, "I appreciate all the amazing things my body allows me to do!"

THINKING BACK AND LOOKING AHEAD

* How did it feel to look at your reflection?
* How did you feel when you said things you appreciate about your body?
* When would it be helpful for us to do this again?
* How can I help you remember all the things you appreciate about your body?

POWER STANCE

Learning about a confident body posture will help kids understand how their posture impacts their mood, feelings, and willingness to try new things or stand up for themselves. When kids feel more confident, they're more loving toward themselves and willing to advocate for their own needs.

Age Range:	**5–11**
Skills:	**Self-reflection**
Materials:	**Mirror**
Number of Participants:	**1+**
Where to Play:	**Anywhere with a tall mirror**

BEFORE YOU START

★ Talk about what it means to have confident body posture. This means that we stand in a way that shows people we believe in ourselves. We can do this by:
  - Standing up tall
  - Keeping our shoulders back
  - Looking up
  - Smiling
★ Talk about times when kids might want to have confident body posture, like:
  - When we are asking for something we need
  - When we stand up for ourselves or others
  - When we give a speech or performance in front of others

HOW TO PLAY

★ Stand in front of a mirror with your child.
★ Practice confident body-posture poses. You can help your child do this with some prompting:
  - Stand like you're feeling really brave!
  - Stand like people are looking up to you!
  - Stand like you're ready to save the day!
★ Ask your child to choose their favorite power stance.

(continued on next page)

THINKING BACK AND LOOKING AHEAD

★ How did it feel to see your power stance in your reflection?

★ When do you think you might use your power stance?

★ How is it different from how you normally stand?

★ How will you feel when you use your power stance in the future?

SELF-LOVE CALENDAR

How can you remind your child to show their body, mind, and spirit some love? Schedule it in until it becomes a habit! Create a calendar of self-love activities and statements to help your child make showing themselves some love a routine.

Age Range:	**5–11**
Skills:	**Creativity, organization, self-care**
Materials:	**Calendar or paper, writing utensil**
Number of Participants:	**1+**
Where to Play:	**Inside**

BEFORE YOU START

★ Talk about what self-care is. You could say, "Self-care includes all the activities we do to promote our physical, mental, emotional, and social health. Self-care activities help us feel cared for and comfortable."

HOW TO PLAY

★ With your child, make a calendar of self-love activities. For younger children, start with just a week of activities. If your child is older, try two weeks or even a whole month.
★ On a calendar or paper, write one activity per day. Here are examples:
  • Write a nice note to myself.
  • Do an exercise I love to take care of my body.
  • Prepare a fun, healthy snack.
  • Take a photo in my favorite outfit.
  • Celebrate a small victory.
★ Help your child complete their self-love activity each day.

THINKING BACK AND LOOKING AHEAD

★ How does it feel to do one thing to show yourself love every day?
★ What self-love activity was your favorite?
★ How do these activities impact your whole day?
★ What other activities would you like to do?

SELF-LOVE TWISTER

Here's a *twist* on a family favorite! Add a little self-love to a game of Twister. When your child lands on a certain color, they'll share something that builds self-love. This fun game will give your child an opportunity to think about the ways they love themselves and are worthy of good things—while doing something physical.

Age Range:	**5–11**
Skills:	**Creativity, self-reflection**
Materials:	**Twister game, paper, writing utensil**
Number of Participants:	**2+**
Where to Play:	**Inside**

BEFORE YOU START

* Review the rules of the game with all the players.
* Set guidelines for each color. You can use these or create your own:
  * Red: Share a strength you have.
  * Blue: Share a way you are kind to others.
  * Green: Share a way you are kind to yourself.
  * Yellow: Share a challenge you overcame that you are proud of.
* Write the color guidelines on paper for everyone to reference throughout the game.

HOW TO PLAY

* Play Twister!
* When someone spins to a color, they will follow the color guideline you set as a group before they complete the movement indicated on the spinner.

THINKING BACK AND LOOKING AHEAD

* What did you enjoy about this game?
* What was difficult about it?
* How did it feel to share these things while we played?

★ What was it like to hear what other players shared?

★ How can we share more about these things in everyday life?

You can also do this activity with many other board games you may have on hand at home—not just Twister! Any game that has color spaces will do. Just assign something to share to all the colors in the game that you have. You can play with any of these family favorites:

* Uno

* Candy Land

* Trouble

* The Game of Life

* Go Fish (assign to suits of the cards)

BREATH MEDITATION

Everyone should take a minute to breathe! This breath meditation helps kids learn to use controlled breathing as a calming and affirming tool. Add in mindful affirmations and you have a recipe for self-love breath meditation.

Age Range:	**5–11**
Skills:	**Self-awareness, mindfulness**
Materials:	**None**
Number of Participants:	**1+**
Where to Play:	**In a quiet, comfortable place free from distractions**

BEFORE YOU START

★ Talk about what self-love is. You could say something like, "Self-love is a practice of loving yourself without judgment. Self-love is accepting yourself exactly the way you are and showing yourself love."

★ Practice controlled breathing with your child. Model a slow inhale and even slower exhale, filling your lungs completely and blowing all the air out completely. For younger children, you can breathe in for a count of 1, 2, 3 and breathe out for a count of 1, 2, 3, 4, 5. Older children may be able to breathe in for a count of 1, 2, 3, 4, 5 and breathe out for a count of 1, 2, 3, 4, 5, 6, 7. If this practice is new or uncomfortable to your child right now, there are lots of controlled-breathing videos for kids available online so they can get comfortable with the practice.

HOW TO PLAY

★ Sit or lie comfortably with your child in a space without distractions.

★ Simply begin breathing with your child using the instructions in the Before You Start section.

* After about ten slow, deep breaths, say an affirmation after the exhale for your child to repeat. You can use affirmations like:
  * I am worthy.
  * I deserve love.
  * I matter.
  * I love myself.
* Have your child end their breathing exercise with a self-hug by squeezing themselves in a hug on the inhale and slowly releasing the hug on the exhale.

THINKING BACK AND LOOKING AHEAD
* How did it feel to slowly breathe like this?
* How did you feel when you said these affirmations?
* In which situations do you think this practice could help you remember your worth?

HOBBIES FOR FUN

When the pressure to be the best at activities can seem like it's rising for kids, having hobbies that are just for fun can offer some balance. Spending time doing hobbies they enjoy just for the fun of them can help kids develop an understanding of self-care and learn to show themselves love by participating in things they enjoy...without the pressure of competition.

Age Range:	5–11
Skills:	Self-care
Materials:	Situationally dependent
Number of Participants:	1+
Where to Play:	Inside, outside, or virtually

BEFORE YOU START

* Talk about what hobbies are. You could say something like, "Hobbies are activities we do that we enjoy. It can be things like doodling, biking, hiking, bird-watching, or something else."
* Talk about what self-care is. You could say something like, "Self-care includes all the activities we do to promote our physical, mental, emotional, and social health. Self-care activities help us feel cared for and comfortable."
* Explain how enjoying hobbies can be a way to engage in self-care. You could say something like, "Taking time for the things we enjoy helps us feel good, center ourselves, and let go of the pressures that we experience at school, on sports teams, and in other competitive settings. Hobbies can just be for fun. We don't have to be the best at them to enjoy them."

HOW TO PLAY

* Talk about hobbies that your child enjoys or would like to try.
* Set aside dedicated time in the family schedule for your child to do their hobbies.

* Resist the urge to encourage them to be the best or turn the hobby into a competition unless your child is highly motivated to do this on their own. Just let it be a hobby for self-care.

THINKING BACK AND LOOKING AHEAD

* How do you feel when you do your hobby?
* What do you love about it?
* How does taking time for yourself and the activities you enjoy change your mood?
* How can I help you make time for the things you enjoy doing?

NEW SKILL DAY

Trying and learning something new is a great confidence builder for kids (and adults) of any age! Add New Skill Day to your family calendar and spend the day trying and learning something new. The experience of learning something new and having success will help your child feel confident in their capacity to grow. Encouraging them to speak kindly to themselves throughout the practice will also be a gentle reminder of the love they deserve along the way.

Age Range:	**5–11**
Skills:	**Task initiation, perseverance**
Materials:	**Situationally dependent**
Number of Participants:	**The whole family**
Where to Play:	**Inside, outside, or virtually**

BEFORE YOU START

★ Together with your family, make a list of new skills you all might like to try or learn. It could be things like:
  • Throwing a curveball
  • Sewing a button
  • Baking chocolate chip cookies
  • Writing in cursive
  • Drawing a horse
  • Climbing a rock wall
★ Talk about how it feels to try something new. You could say something like, "Sometimes it's exciting! Sometimes it can be a little frustrating when it isn't easy right away. But when we keep trying or try new strategies, we get better! We can also speak kindly to ourselves as we try to help ourselves feel confident and stay motivated."

HOW TO PLAY

★ Gather the necessary materials or plan the outing that is necessary for the skill your family wants to try.

★ On your designated New Skill Day, set aside time to try the skill. Watch videos of others doing the activity or teaching the skill, or teach your child the skill yourself. If your child has an older sibling or cousin who can teach them a skill, invite them along! Learning from people they care about will be motivating, and knowing others want to impart knowledge will help kids feel cared for (and teaching someone something new will offer a self-love boost for the teacher too!).

★ Practice the skill for the time that you have, and then reflect on the experience.

THINKING BACK AND LOOKING AHEAD

★ What was it like to try this new skill today?

★ Did it go how you expected? Why or why not?

★ How did you feel when you weren't successful right away? How did you motivate yourself to keep going? What strategies did you try?

★ How did it feel when you were successful?

★ What did you say to yourself to encourage yourself?

★ What other new skills do you want to try on our next New Skill Day?

Make a list of phrases your child can say to themselves when they try a new skill and it doesn't come easily right away. It might look something like this:

• It's okay not to be great at new things on the first try.

• What other strategy could I try?

• This is challenging! But I've overcome challenges before.

• It's okay to ask for help.

• Learning new things can be fun if I don't put a lot of pressure on myself.

• Challenges make me stronger!

HEART BANNER

This sweet banner will remind kids of all the reasons they love themselves. Making this visual representation of their self-love a part of everyday decor will help them focus on it on a daily basis.

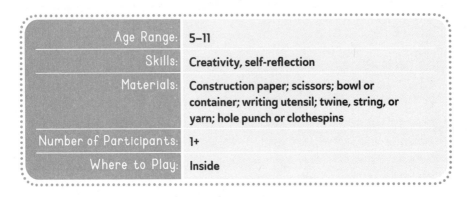

Age Range:	5–11
Skills:	Creativity, self-reflection
Materials:	Construction paper; scissors; bowl or container; writing utensil; twine, string, or yarn; hole punch or clothespins
Number of Participants:	1+
Where to Play:	Inside

BEFORE YOU START
* Cut out paper hearts that are large enough to write a short sentence on. Place them in a bowl or container.

HOW TO PLAY
* Kids will write reasons they love themselves on the paper hearts. Younger kids might need help writing. This can be done all in one sitting, or it can be something they do daily or when they think of something they love.
* When your child has ten or more hearts, string them on a piece of twine, string, or yarn. You can punch holes in the hearts with a hole punch to string them or clip the hearts to the string with clothespins.
* Hang the self-love banner in your child's room.
* Continue doing this for every ten hearts they make over time for a visual display of self-love.

THINKING BACK AND LOOKING AHEAD
* What is it like to think about the reasons you love yourself?
* How do you feel when you look at the banner?
* How can I help remind you of all the reasons you love yourself?

SELF-LOVE YOGA SEQUENCE

Take time to practice these peaceful poses with uplifting affirmations to remind your child that their body is strong and they are worthy of love! This practice will help kids focus on what they can do with their bodies and incorporate self-love affirmations into their daily lives.

Age Range:	5–11
Skills:	Flexibility, concentration, mindfulness
Materials:	Yoga mats (optional)
Number of Participants:	1+
Where to Play:	In an open space free from distractions

BEFORE YOU START

★ Talk about what yoga is and some of the benefits of it. You can say something like, "Yoga is an ancient practice that involves posing your body, breathing deeply, and concentrating on your body and movements. Yoga can help us feel calm, strong, and peaceful."

HOW TO PLAY

★ Create an open space free from distractions for a yoga practice with your child. If you have yoga mats, place these on the floor. Begin your yoga practice together using these poses and affirmations (older kids might want to say the affirmations to themselves):
  • Mountain Pose: Stand tall with your feet flat on the ground, hip-width distance apart. Place your arms straight beside your body with your palms facing forward. Say together, "I am strong like a mighty mountain." Hold this pose for 30–60 seconds.
  • Star Pose: Step your feet wide and spread your arms out as wide as your feet with palms facing forward. Say together, "I shine bright like a star." Hold this pose for 30–60 seconds.

(continued on next page)

- Warrior Pose: Step one foot forward in front of the other, bending the front knee and keeping the back leg straight. Hold your arms straight above your head with your palms facing each other. Say together, "I am brave like a warrior." Hold this pose for 30–60 seconds and repeat on the other side.
- Tree Pose: Place your feet flat on the ground with your legs hip-width distance apart. Bend one knee out, then place your foot on the inside of the other ankle, calf, or thigh. Raise your hands straight above your head with palms facing each other. Say together, "I am firmly rooted in who I am." Hold this pose for 30–60 seconds and repeat on the other side.
- Mountain Pose: Return to Mountain Pose. Stand tall with your feet flat on the ground, hip-width distance apart. Place your arms straight beside your body with your palms facing forward. Say together, "I am strong like a mighty mountain." Hold this pose for 30–60 seconds.
- Savasana: Lie flat on your back on your yoga mat (if using) with your legs out straight and arms flat on the ground beside your body, palms facing up. Say together, "I can allow myself to rest to take care of my body." Hold this pose for 60 seconds.

★ Bring your arms up in a hug around your chest. Say together, "I can show myself the love I deserve." Hold this pose for 60 seconds.

THINKING BACK AND LOOKING AHEAD
★ How did it feel to do this yoga sequence?
★ Which pose was your favorite? Why?
★ Which affirmation was your favorite? Why?
★ When do you think we could incorporate this into our daily routine? How would it help you to do this more often?

Research tells us that yoga has a whole host of benefits for kids! Practicing yoga helps kids with emotion regulation and anxiety management. It can also improve kids' body awareness. strength. flexibility. concentration. and memory. Research also suggests that regularly practicing yoga helps kids reduce impulsivity. Making this a regular practice will pay dividends for social. behavioral. emotional. and academic growth!

AFFIRMATION ALPHABET

In this activity, you'll spend some time with your child creating an affirmation that starts with every letter of the alphabet. Creating a list of creative affirmations will help your child call to mind positive words when they need them to restore their physical or mental well-being.

Age Range:	7–11
Skills:	Creativity, self-care
Materials:	Paper, pencil, coloring utensils (optional), picture frame (optional)
Number of Participants:	1+
Where to Play:	Inside

BEFORE YOU START

★ Talk about what an affirmation is. You could say something like, "An affirmation is a statement or sentence that we say to ourselves to build ourselves up, encourage ourselves, or remind ourselves of strengths and values. Saying or reading affirmations can make us feel good about ourselves, and affirmations can help us focus on the good within ourselves, especially when things feel hard or challenging."

HOW TO PLAY

★ On paper, write the alphabet from A to Z vertically on the left side of the page. If your child wants to, let them add an illustration or symbol beside each letter or simply make a creative border or block letters to make the A-to-Z affirmation list beautiful!
★ For each letter, create an affirmation that starts with that letter. Here are a few examples:
  • A: Accept yourself. You are amazing the way you are!
  • B: Be brave. You can do hard things!
  • C: Choose kindness. Be kind to yourself and others.
★ This activity can be an ongoing challenge or something you create in an afternoon or weekend.

(continued on next page)

* When you are finished, hang it somewhere highly visible or frame it for your child.
* Each day, choose one affirmation to say together!

THINKING BACK AND LOOKING AHEAD
* What was it like to create these affirmations?
* Which one is your favorite?
* How do you feel when you say these affirmations?

BLOCK LETTER NAME

Your name is a representation of yourself. Fill the letters of your name with positive traits and qualities you have to remind yourself of all the amazing things to love about you.

Age Range:	**7–11**
Skills:	**Creativity, self-reflection**
Materials:	**Paper, pencil, picture frame (optional), coloring utensils**
Number of Participants:	**1+**
Where to Play:	**Inside**

BEFORE YOU START
* Get a list of positive qualities, traits, or skills. You can find alphabetized lists online.
* Talk about positive qualities your child has. Focus more on traits and qualities over physical appearances (e.g., "kind" and "curious" over "pretty" and "cute").

HOW TO PLAY
* On paper, help your child write their name in block letters. They can color or decorate these letters if they want.
* Inside the block letters, help your child write positive qualities they possess that start with the same letters in their name. For example, you could write "dedicated," "diligent," and "dog lover" within the D in "Diego."
* Display the paper somewhere highly visible, or frame it for your child to see often.

THINKING BACK AND LOOKING AHEAD
* What was it like to think about your positive qualities?
* How will you feel when you see your block letter name?
* What other qualities would you add?

GRATITUDE TREE

I'm grateful for my body! Create a gratitude tree, with a twist. Reflect on reasons you're grateful to be in your body to plant strong roots of self-love.

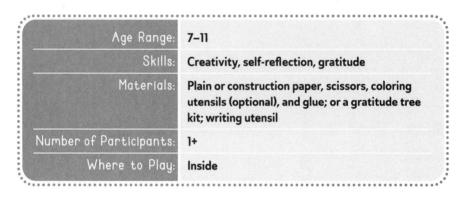

Age Range:	**7–11**
Skills:	**Creativity, self-reflection, gratitude**
Materials:	**Plain or construction paper, scissors, coloring utensils (optional), and glue; or a gratitude tree kit; writing utensil**
Number of Participants:	**1+**
Where to Play:	**Inside**

BEFORE YOU START

* Talk about what it means to be grateful. You could say something like, "'Grateful' means that we appreciate something, someone, some experiences, some qualities, and so on."
* Talk about reasons to be grateful for all the things your body does for you. You can say, "We can be grateful for our strong bones, smart brain, hardworking muscles, and so much more!"

HOW TO PLAY

* Using plain or construction paper, make a tree trunk, branches, and leaf shapes. Cut these shapes out of paper and have your child color them in if they'd like. Then glue the branches to the trunk. Or, if you'd like, use a gratitude tree kit to construct the tree and branches.
* On the leaves, help your child write reasons they are grateful for their body.
* Glue the leaves onto the branches.
* Display the gratitude tree somewhere highly visible so your child can see it often.

THINKING BACK AND LOOKING AHEAD

★ What was it like to think about reasons you're grateful for your body?

★ Which one of these reasons is most meaningful to you?

★ When will it be helpful for you to look at your gratitude tree?

★ How can I help you remember the reasons you are grateful for your body?

SELF-CARE CHECKLIST

What's the ultimate way to show yourself self-love? Self-care! In this activity, kids will make a list of activities they need to complete in order to feel cared for and comfortable. Whether it's physical, emotional, or mental in nature, self-care is a habit that should start when you're young.

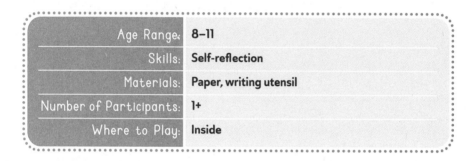

Age Range:	**8–11**
Skills:	**Self-reflection**
Materials:	**Paper, writing utensil**
Number of Participants:	**1+**
Where to Play:	**Inside**

BEFORE YOU START

★ Talk about what self-care is. You could say something like, "Self-care includes all the activities we do to promote our physical, mental, emotional, and social health. Self-care activities help us feel cared for and comfortable."

HOW TO PLAY

★ Brainstorm a list of self-care activities for kids. Here are some ideas to get you started (there are lots of lists available online if you need more ideas!):
  • Spend time in nature every day
  • Write in my journal
  • Take a relaxing bath
  • Spend time doodling
  • Listen to a favorite audiobook
  • Spend time with a friend
  • Talk about my feelings
★ With your child, check off or highlight the self-care activities that they enjoy or need to complete in order to feel cared for and comfortable.
★ Display the list somewhere highly visible! Or use this list to create the Self-Love Calendar discussed earlier in this chapter and help your child stay on track with their self-care.

THINKING BACK AND LOOKING AHEAD

★ How do these activities help your body and mind feel cared for?

★ Which of the activities is hard for you to remember to do?

★ Which of these activities is easiest for you to remember to do?

★ How can I help you stay on track with self-care?

THOUGHT FLIPPING

Does your child have negative thoughts about themselves? It's time to flip them! Thought flipping is a cognitive behavioral therapy technique used to change the way we feel about ourselves. When your child has negative thoughts about their body, abilities, or interests, help them flip those thoughts to see themselves in a more positive and gentle light.

Age Range:	8–11
Skills:	Self-reflection
Materials:	None
Number of Participants:	1+
Where to Play:	Inside

BEFORE YOU START

★ Talk about what it means to be gentle with yourself. You could say something like, "Being gentle means that we act with kindness and caution so that we don't hurt others or things. But we can be gentle with ourselves too! We can act carefully and with self-control to keep our bodies safe, but we can also be gentle with our words. We can speak kindly and gently to ourselves so that we remember that we are worthy, we are growing, and we deserve love."

HOW TO PLAY

★ When your child says something negative about themselves or shares a negative thought they have about themselves, help them flip the thought in a more positive and realistic way. Here are a few examples:
  • Negative thought: I'll never be any good at this.
  • Flipped thought: This is hard right now. I have gotten better at other things when I've kept trying.
  • Negative thought: Everyone is judging me and thinks I'm weird.
  • Flipped thought: Most people are thinking about themselves, not me. I like who I am.

* When using thought flipping, it's important that the new thought is realistic and not just purely positive. Using realistic self-talk will help kids see themselves in a gentler way and help them develop love for who they are right now.

THINKING BACK AND LOOKING AHEAD
* How do you feel when you have that negative thought? How does it impact your day?
* How do you feel when you say the flipped thought?
* How can I help you remember to flip thoughts when you are thinking or feeling negatively about yourself?

SELF-LOVE PLAYLIST

What songs lift you up? Create a playlist of songs that remind your child of their worth and lift their spirits—and encourage them to move their body! The words kids hear—whether from others, themselves, music, or the world—help shape their inner self-talk. Positive, uplifting music will help that inner dialogue be positive and remind them of their worth.

Age Range:	**8–11**
Skills:	**Mindfulness**
Materials:	**Music, music player**
Number of Participants:	**1+**
Where to Play:	**Inside or virtually**

BEFORE YOU START

★ Talk about how the things we watch and listen to and the conversations we have with others impact our thoughts and our outlook. You could say something like, "When we listen to or watch positive things or when we speak positively with others, we think more positively about the world and ourselves. We can help ourselves feel more positive and loving toward ourselves and the world by putting positive words into our minds!"

HOW TO PLAY

★ Together with your child, make a playlist of songs they enjoy that are positive and uplifting. Here are some ideas to get you started:
  - "Brave" by Sara Bareilles
  - "Count on Me" by Bruno Mars
  - "Fight Song" by Rachel Platten
  - "Get Back Up Again" on the *Trolls* soundtrack
  - "How Far I'll Go" on the *Moana* soundtrack
  - "I'm Still Standing" on the *Sing* soundtrack
  - "Shake It Off" on the *Sing* soundtrack
  - "This Is Me" on *The Greatest Showman* soundtrack

- "True Colors" on the *Trolls* soundtrack
- "What Makes You Beautiful" by One Direction

★ If your child has their own music-playing device, add the playlist to their device for them to listen to.

★ Listen to the playlist together in the car, on bike rides, or just in the home, and dance or sing along!

THINKING BACK AND LOOKING AHEAD

★ How do you feel when you listen to these songs?

★ How do these songs impact your mood? Your day? Your actions?

★ What other songs would you like to add to our playlist?

PRACTICAL APPLICATION

The activities and games included in Part 2 of this book are fun, interactive ways to understand and show self-love, but there is room for growth outside of games too! In Part 3, we will discuss meaningful and practical ways that you can weave self-esteem and self-love development into your everyday life and conversations to encourage kids to better understand themselves and the world around them.

Some of these methods will take time and consistent practice in order to make positive changes. Ongoing practice will give kids the best opportunity for growth and learning that they'll retain. Investing the time in the "long game" will pay off as kids feel comfortable to practice skills in the safety of their family unit.

CHAPTER 11

INCORPORATING SKILLS INTO EVERYDAY LIFE

In the past ten chapters, we've discussed at length what self-esteem is and how it develops; how self-love is a by-product of high self-esteem; components of self-love; and fun, hands-on ways to help your child develop a sense of self-love. Let's take a moment to say this is no easy feat. With factors that are outside our control and influences from the outside world that play a role in the development of self-esteem and subsequent development of self-love, instilling a strong sense of self-love in kids is a big task. But it's one that is so important!

The positive outcomes of having healthy self-esteem and feelings of self-love are undeniable. We want kids to love themselves, practice self-care, set healthy boundaries, assert themselves and stand up for their needs, and reach out for help when they need it. This chapter will examine some practical, everyday ways to give kids a self-love boost.

EVERYDAY SECURITY

A sense of security at home and out in the world is an important component of a child's sense of self. Here are some practical ways to promote that sense of security:

* Create a warm, loving environment. At home, remind kids that they are loved unconditionally. The love they experience early in life will be the model they use for loving themselves later. Spend special time together, show love to your child in the way they prefer, and remind them that you are there to support them.
* Practice active listening. Feeling like they are heard goes a long way in helping kids see that what they have to say matters to you. When kids are talking to you, show them that what they have to say is important to you by eliminating distractions like phones or the TV, making eye contact, and responding to what they have to say.

* **Keep the lines of communication open.** Offer kids time to share things with you each day. This can be a special designated time, like dinnertime or before bed, or an unstructured time when you simply ask if they have anything they want to talk about. When kids do share, be mindful to respond in loving ways that show kids you have their best interest in mind so they are more likely to come to you with communication in the future.
* **Talk about helpers and safety routines.** If kids are aware of dangerous or scary things in the world that challenge their sense of safety, spend some time talking about safety routines or plans for your family (like where to meet in the event of a house fire). Then remind kids that there are helpers in the community who want to create a safe place to live too.

EVERYDAY BELONGING

Promoting a sense of belonging in the family is as simple as reminding kids that they are an important part of your family no matter what. This can also extend beyond the family as kids get older and explore outside of the family unit. Here are some practical ways to promote a sense of belonging:

* **Celebrate your family.** Spend special time together honoring your family. Celebrate big and small wins, start traditions, and involve everyone in the family to ensure they know they have a place.
* **Encourage social engagement.** Whether your child is into sports, arts, music, or playing video games, encourage them to join age-appropriate teams, clubs, or groups. Model positive social engagement by spending time with your own friends and community members so that children see that engagement outside of the family is important too. Belonging in more than one place is totally okay.

EVERYDAY CONFIDENCE

Helping kids build confidence is all about exposing them to new things and offering opportunities for success. Here are some practical ways to promote confidence in everyday life:

* **Offer opportunities for success.** Give your child opportunities to try new things or improve in areas they've already tried. This could look like

working together to practice that free throw shot or taking an online art class together. Simply offering opportunities for growth is the first step to building confidence in new areas.

* **Provide encouraging feedback.** As kids try new things, offer verbal encouragement. Recognize that trying new things is hard and praise them for being willing to try. If you can offer tips for improvement, do it in gentle, uplifting ways so that kids feel like you're there to help them get better, rather than simply pointing out their mistakes.
* **Encourage perseverance.** When new tasks are hard, encourage kids to keep trying. Remind kids of times when something was hard in the past and they got better with time and effort. And remember: It's okay to take a break and come back and try again later!
* **Celebrate small successes.** Take time to honor and celebrate growth along the way. Celebration doesn't only have to be at the very end when achievement or mastery comes. You can celebrate small steps toward success to help kids build confidence to keep going.

EVERYDAY COMPETENCE

Promoting a sense of competence involves offering opportunities for mastery and taking time to acknowledge it when it happens. Here are some practical ways to do both of those things:

* **Offer opportunities for independent success.** Competence means having the skill set to achieve a task. Help kids realize their competence by giving them the chance to independently do tasks whenever possible. This can be as simple as making their own lunch or tying their own shoes, or as involved as applying past learning to complete a big school project.
* **Encourage self-evaluation.** As kids engage in independent tasks, encourage them to take time to evaluate their strategies, their success, and their direction. As they engage in self-evaluation, they'll be more attuned to their skill set, how they're applying their skills, and how they can use their skills to improve.

EVERYDAY PURPOSE AND CONTRIBUTION

Promoting a sense of purpose and contribution requires a little planning but can go a long way. Here are some practical ways to do this:

* **Create opportunities for family contribution.** At home, create ways for kids to contribute to the family. These can be chores or tasks that make life better for others in the family, like offering encouragement, sharing with siblings, or doing tasks that help someone.
* **Link kids' skills to these contributions.** Recognize your child's strengths and find ways to link these to the opportunities for contribution. For example, if your child has great organizational skills, let them plan the family menu for the week. If your child is an artist, encourage them to use this skill to help family members decorate their rooms in ways that make them feel happy.

EVERYDAY INFLUENCE

Promoting a sense of influence comes down to "voice and choice." Here are some practical ways to promote both of those things:

* **Ask for your child's opinion.** In a variety of areas, ask your child for their opinion. This can be about the news story you just watched on TV or what dish you should take to the neighborhood block party. Showing kids that you care about what they think will go a long way in helping them develop a sense of influence.
* **Offer choices.** Whenever possible, offer reasonable choices. When kids feel like they have a say and a sense of control in their environment, they're more likely to positively engage, feel calm and regulated, and feel a sense of security.

EVERYDAY IDENTITY

A child's sense of identity unfolds over time. Here are some practical ways to promote this development in daily life:

* **Talk about family history.** Spend time exploring family history and learning about the stories of other family members. Knowing where they "came from" can help kids develop a clearer picture of who they are today.
* **Interact with other generations and family members.** Spending time with older generations and family members outside the nuclear family can help kids develop a sense of how they fit into a larger community and form ideas about who they want to become. This also

offers opportunities for exploring family morals and values that will help shape how kids view themselves and the world.

* **Let kids try on different identities.** Is it just a phase? Maybe! But that's okay. Let kids try on different identities as they explore who they are and who they want to become. Do they want to join the drama club and embrace the thespian identity? Great! Do they want to learn about classic rock and wear all the old band tees they found in the attic? Wonderful. Do they want to combine aspects of different interests and cultures? Awesome. Let them try on different components of the identity they are exploring so that they can feel safe to understand who they are and who they are becoming.

EVERYDAY WORTH

Promoting a sense of worth starts with pointing out how kids are unconditionally worthy to you. Here are some everyday ways to help kids develop a sense of worth:

* **Practice respect.** Create a culture of respect at home where family members are expected to be respectful of people and things and speak to each other respectfully. This will set the tone for the treatment kids believe they deserve in the world.
* **Practice compassion and forgiveness.** Showing care and compassion to one another in daily life also models for kids what kind of treatment they deserve from others outside the family. Forgiving each other for mistakes models for kids not only how to treat others but also how to treat themselves. Being gentle with each other, recognizing that everyone makes mistakes, and forgiving each other for mistakes is a sure way to help kids develop a sense of self-love!

EVERYDAY PHYSICAL WELL-BEING

Taking care of kids' bodies and minds is an important part of self-love. Here are some everyday ways to help kids develop their physical well-being:

* **Create well-being routines.** Set aside time each day or week for activities that promote a healthy lifestyle. This could be a family walk, making a nourishing meal together, or another enjoyed activity.

* **Try new forms of movement.** Rather than focusing on terms like *exercise* and *workout*, encourage your child to simply find movement that feels good and that they enjoy. Try jumping rope, hula hooping, rock climbing, skating, or something new so that they are exposed to many types of movement and can find a fun way to move their body. It won't feel like a chore if they genuinely enjoy it.
* **Practice family self-care.** Build self-care practices into your everyday family life and honor them. Showing your child the importance of caring for their mental, physical, emotional, social, and spiritual health goes a long way in reminding them that they are worthy of love and care.

SELF-LOVE FOR LIFE

Self-love is an important part of taking care of your physical, mental, emotional, social, and spiritual needs; setting boundaries; asserting yourself; forming strong, meaningful relationships; and so much more. The self-awareness, self-reflection, mindfulness, and problem-solving that go into developing self-love are critical skills for many areas of life. The love that kids develop for themselves—and the actions they learn to take to show themselves love and respect—can help them grow into healthy, happy adults.

Self-love starts with the belief that you are worthy of love and continues with the actions that demonstrate love and care toward yourself. Self-love looks and feels a little different to each person, and that's okay. Use the activities in this book to enrich your relationship with your child and model for them the love they deserve and can show to themselves throughout their lifetime! Enjoy your time growing in love together.

INDEX